D1311438

Freedom

vs

Socialism

Dr. Alexander G. Alemis

ISBN : 9781671279223

Contact the Author

DrAlemis.com

A Note about the Cover

Adam Smith (left): A Scottish philosopher and economist (1723-1790). Mr. Smith became well known for his most famous work, **The Wealth of Nations**. He was a strong proponent of the free market economy and today is considered the **"The Father of Capitalism."** (Encyclopedia Britannica)

Karl Marx (right)**:** A German Philosopher and Economist (1818-1883), best known for his works, **The Communist Manifesto and Das Kapital**, two anti-free enterprise pieces. He is considered **"The Father of Communism."** (Encyclopedia Britannica)

These descriptions for of each economist are considered gospel in today's world, yet neither man was father of what the world assigns them to be.

Adam Smith was an advocate of free enterprise and not capitalism as is known today. He only considered mining and agricultural products (things which come from the earth) as part of the legitimate economy, not commerce and certainly not the stock market. Most notable though is that the "Father of Capitalism" never owned a company, never got married and he lived in his mother's house for most of his life. In reality he was the antithesis of free enterprise which involves creation and risk taking.

Karl Marx never put his theories to application to see if they worked or not. He was a heavy drinker, both his daughters committed suicide and very few people showed up to his funeral, so he was really an unknown. The reason Mr. Marx grew a long beard (see picture) was an attempt to emulate the ancient Greek god Zeus, personified in a statue he saw, whom he admired greatly*. So, the world's greatest "equalitarian" was a big admirer of the least equalitarian of all the personas of the ancient world.

*See the "The making of modern economics", Mark Skousen, Third Edition Page 148

Table of Contents

ACKNOWLEDGEMENTS

I dedicate this work to all the true freedom fighters around the world and throughout history. The ones who advocate that the free enterprise system in a responsible democracy is the only political system which provides freedom for the human spirit to create and be happy.

To my father who was a true believer in free enterprise and saw to it that I come to America.

To my uncle, James Alemis, who was here to accept and support me.

To my family who support me in all my endeavors. My wife Tina and my children, Peter, Katerina and Constantine.

To my staff Laura Pugh and Irene Torrez for tirelessly typing, retyping, editing, and reediting this book as it was developing, among their many other duties.

MY PHILOSOPHY

The Political System which exists in a country is what determines the success or failure of that country and its citizens.

Some say that you can succeed in any economy or political system. That is like saying, "Ignore the cobra or tiger in the corner. If you pretend they are not there, they will not bite you."

Responsible democracy and true free-enterprise is the best governing system ever developed. It takes what naturally exists in the world and it arranges it in the most optimal manner to create the most possible success and happiness for the people in it.

MY MISSION

People ask me why I have embarked on this journey of writing books on politics and economics. After all, I am a doctor, not a politician or an economist. To that, I answer: "It seems I was born asking the question:

WHAT IS THE MOST OPTIMAL SYSTEM FOR THE

BEST GOVERNANCE OF PEOPLE IN ANY SOCIETY?"

Therefore, my mission has been to discover, document and promote the most optimal system of governance.

Not to compare myself with Thomas Jefferson in any way, but following is an excerpt from a letter he sent to a friend which I find befitting.

"We have both been drawn from our natural passion for study and tranquility, by times which took from us the freedom of choice: times however which, planting a new world with the seeds of just government, will produce a remarkable era in the history of mankind. It was incumbent on those therefore who fell into them, to give up every favorite pursuit, and lay their shoulder to the work of the day."

-Thomas Jefferson

HOW TO READ THIS BOOK

You must read this book by posing the question: **What is different here, and why would it work when other systems have failed?** This is not a book that regurgitates information from other books. The thoughts and ideas presented here are unique and not found in any other literature.

In my not so humble opinion, I believe that this book contains all the theory anyone needs to know about the different political systems and how they relate to freedom, democracy and the economy. The astute reader, after reading this book in depth, will come out knowing more about the subject than political science professors in universities who are loaded with theories and significances. But a word of caution to the cursory reader. Please realize that as you read this book, you will come up against assertions, beliefs or ideas which you will find objectionable or that are one sided. I believe that those concerns, questions and disagreements will be answered fully on the subsequent chapters. Therefore, it is imperative to read this book fully, before you form an opinion about it, and make sure you clear all misunderstood words that you come across in it.

EXPERT ON OBSERVATION AND CONNECTING THE DOTS

When my son invited a friend to my lecture on the presentation of this book, the friend inquired: "Is Dr. Alemis an expert on socialism?" So my son asked me on how he should respond. I told him to tell his friend that; I am not a humanities expert, but a scientist, and that I consider myself an expert on observation and connecting the dots much differently than other people."

The main problems with "the humanities experts" as opposed to the physical scientists are as follows:

1. They do not measure the results of their theories to see if they work or not, as for example in education.
2. They are mostly unable to observe for themselves, but regurgitate other "experts" work because, they would rather be "wrong than alone".

I do not suffer from the above "afflictions" as you can see from all of my books.

In terms of connecting the dots differently, here are some of my observation stories:

1. When I was in grammar school in Europe, World War II covered a large part of our history lesson. At one point during the lecture, I asked my teacher the following question: "Why was Switzerland not involved in the war

yet it was in the middle of everything and next to Germany?" My teacher's answer was: "Because they were neutral." I was eleven years old then, but I knew that he had given me a no answer.

Have you ever wondered how the Swiss stayed "neutral" from both sides? The Allies could have used them to invade Germany from there and the Germans could have invaded Switzerland to protect themselves or to loot them. No one seems to ever address this obvious puzzling question about World War II.

2. The world's finances are supposedly run by "experts". Those "experts" have run the world into massive debt. See below, a Bloomberg report (January 2019). When I have confronted some of them about this nonsensical handling of finance, they have given me answers which they have read elsewhere, but make no sense. It is my humble opinion that these people are not experts despite what their diplomas state, at least not on finance.

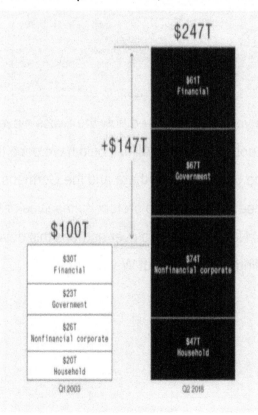

3. In the spring of 2017 I was having lunch at a restaurant downtown Athens after one of my lectures, and as I looked out I saw a face on the Acropolis rock. See following pictures. After checking with "experts" (Greek archeologists) who worked specifically on and about the Acropolis, they told me that they have never seen this carving before. How on earth is this possible from all these "experts" who have studied the Acropolis for over 2,000 years?

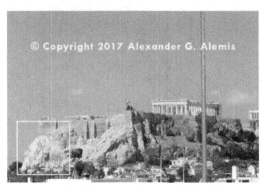

Google or see YouTube: Dr. Alemis the face on the Acropolis

4. When my daughter was in high school, she read in her history books written "by experts" that women in ancient Greece were treated as second-class citizens. So, I did my own research on the subject and showed her a myriad of Greek statues which show the women at the same status as man. I also stumbled upon the artifact shown below in one of the encyclopedias. This clearly shows a teenage girl being led to school by her mother somewhere in ancient Athens. I told my daughter to look at their dresses, their hair and their overall appearance. Also to observe the girl's books and stylus and then decide if women in ancient Greece were treated as second-class citizens when half the world's teenage girls today (2,500 years later) have not reached the level depicted on this ancient artifact.

New York
Metropolitan
Museum of Art

Accession
Number:
06.1021.167

My daughter was surprised about what I showed her and she did not trust these "experts" anymore.

INTRODUCTION

There have been thousands of books comparing different political systems. So why another one? Well, as you read the following pages, you will see a comparative analysis that is different, yet far simpler and much more basic, than any books you might have read on the subject. After reading this book you will come away with a much better understanding of the different political systems and ways of governance that exist in our society today and throughout the ages. Also you will have an understanding of the differences between Free Enterprise[1,] True Free Enterprise,[2] Capitalism[3], Democracy[4]and any of the totalitarian systems[5] such as fascisms[6] or socialism[7] leading to communism[7].

A more accurate and befitting title for this book would have been:

"FREE ENTERPRISE VERSUS TOTALITARIAN SYSTEMS".

Unfortunately, most people don't know the meaning of the word totalitarian, and *Freedom Versus Socialism,* rated better in the surveys.

1. **Free Enterprise**: The economic doctrine or practice of permitting private industry to operate under freely competitive conditions with a minimum of governmental control. (Webster's New World College Dictionary, Fourth Edition)

My Definition of free enterprise: A system which encourages people to bring forth their ideas to the market and be allowed to compete against other ideas and systems. For example, Ray Kroc (founder of McDonalds) had an idea for a system on how to prepare and serve hamburgers which was different than other restaurants and was allowed to compete and test his system in the market against other ideas of making and serving food, mainly hamburgers. He created his own company and was allowed to own the enterprise and benefit from the services it provided.

2. **A true free enterprise system** (my definition) is a free enterprise system as above but **where there are no monopolies or oligopolies in it** and there is limited interference and taxations from the government. *In a true free enterprise system people are mainly rewarded for the creation and the exchange of products and services.* The stock market can be part of the true free enterprise system as long as it supports products and services and it's not a Ponzi Scheme created by fake money (government printed) or fake demand, such as when central banks or the government buy stocks of companies they want to support, for whatever reason, directly or indirectly.

3. **Capitalism**: An economic system in which all or most of the means of production and distribution, as land, factories,

communications, and transportation systems are privately owned and operated in a relatively competitive environment through the investment of capital to produce profits. It has been characterized by a tendency toward the concentration of wealth, the growth of large corporations, etc. that has led to economic inequality which has been dealt with usually by increased government action and control (Webster's New World College Dictionary)

My definitions of capitalism:

1. An economic system which encompasses free enterprise, but allows monopolies or oligopolies to develop and stifle true free enterprise.

2. It is the use of money by people in power to profit without the emphasis being on the creation and exchange of products and/or services. Examples of this would be when:

    a) A law restricts competition to one's business

    b) The manipulation of world events and the consequent flipping of currencies for profit.

    c) Favoritism from government connections and the ability to use tax payers' money and/or the receiving of money from central banks.

3. **A word coined by Karl Marx describing a perverted definition of free enterprise. People today superimpose the definition of free enterprise with capitalism and**

mistakenly think as you see from the previous definitions they are the same.

4. **Democracy.** My definitions:

1. It comes from two words, **Demos** which means citizenry and **Kratos** which means rule or law. It is a political system based on the citizens of a country having a say so in their governance. Democracy was first developed in ancient Greece and predominantly Athens. It contributed to the Golden Age of Greece and to the American civilization as it copied Athenian Democracy with an American flare. **Democracy, as explained in the book *Political Systems and Their Relationship to the Economy and Freedom,* is the most important thing ever developed for mankind.** As such, the word Democracy is thrown around like candy to appease people. Most totalitarian countries call themselves democracies. **True democracy in a true free enterprise system is very rare in human history. It's the stuff of dreams and Golden Ages.**

2. It's the opposite of a totalitarian system.

5. **A Totalitarian Political system,** is defined as:

a: of or relating to centralized control by an autocratic leader or hierarchy b: of or relating to a political regime based on subordination of the individual to the state and strict control of all aspects of the life and productive capacity of the nation especially by coercive measures (such as censorship and terrorism) (Merriam Webster)

My definitions: 1. Totalitarian=all in one, meaning: all power is concentrated in one group or one person and it's the opposite of democracy. 2. Fascism and Communism are the best examples of totalitarian systems in our world today.

5. Fascism *often capitalized* : a political philosophy, movement, or regime (such as that of the Fascist) that exalts nation and often race, above the individual, and that stands for a centralized autocratic government headed by a dictatorial leader, severe economic and social regimentation, and forcible suppression of opposition (Meriam Webster)

6. Socialism is defined as

a. any of various economic and political theories advocating collective or governmental ownership and administration of the means of production and distribution of goods

b. a system of society or group living in which there is no private property

c. a system or condition of society in which the means of production are owned and controlled by the state

d. a stage of society in Marxist theory **transitional** between capitalism and communism and distinguished by unequal distribution of goods and pay according to work done (Merriam Webster)

My emphasis, on the word transitional. This is critical to understanding socialism for what it truly is. Marx correctly called socialism a transitional state with its ultimate goal being communism.

7. **Communism** is defined as: A system in which goods are owned in common*and are available to all as needed. A theory advocating the **elimination** of private property (Merriam Webster)

*Meaning that the government owns and controls "your share of goods," for your "own benefit," so they claim, as they pretend to know what is best for you. In essence though, in communism you own nothing, not even your own body or thoughts (my comments).

I can spend a lot more time defining these political concepts/systems, but they will become more clear to you as you read the rest of the book.

In our world today, there are no absolute free enterprise democracies or totalitarian systems, but rather many degrees and

20

shades of each. **Most countries are closer to totalitarian systems than true free enterprise democracies, thus the importance of this book.**

The so-called capitalistic democracies of the Western World countries, comprise mostly of Oligopolies[1], if not practical monopolies[2] despite the anti-trust laws in the books. **Monopolies and oligopolies bring about the rise of socialism,** more on that in the book chapters.

A graphic categorization of all the systems above is done in the book: ***Political Systems and Their Relationship to the Economy and Freedom.*** The following page is an excerpt from that book. **It is a unique graphic depiction of the different political systems as they relate to the economy and freedom.** The numbers 100 to -10 are arbitrary. For more graphs, see above book.

---

[1]   Oligopolies: Oligo= few, Politis=seller A market situation in which only a few companies control a particular market

[2]   Monopolies: Mono=one, Politis=seller. When one company controls an entire market

GRAPHIC DEPICTIONS OF POLITICAL SYSTEMS AS THEY

RELATE TO THE ECONOMY AND FREEDOM

(From ideal to chaos)

Survivability Potential	Economic System	Political System	Individual Freedom	Chances of Tyrannical Government
100	TRUE FREE ENTERPRISE	Responsible Democracy By Educated Citizens	Most Freedom	Very Low
70	OLIGOPOLIES AND BIG GOVERNMENT	Irresponsible Democracy		
50	MONOPOLIES AND SOCIALISM		Less Freedom	
40	SOCIALISM	Perverted Democracy		
20	FASCISM	No Democracy	No Freedom	
10	COMMUNISM			
0		No Government		100%
-10	ANARCHY	Chaos	Chaos	Gangs Rule

When in anarchy, people demand totalitarian systems, thus the arrows pointing upward.

When I first showed this graph at one of my seminars, people were quick to point out that it did not cover a kingship or a theocracy. My position on these two "systems" is that they still fall under these categories. You can have a king who is pro free enterprise and democracy or one who is very tyrannical. Same is true for any political systems run by religious leaders as in the past or present. They can be pro-freedom and free enterprise or fascistic and very restrictive to personal freedoms.

In short, any political system or religious philosophy for all practical purposes would fall somewhere on this graph and should be judged as such, i.e. based on its behavior and not by its name.

Another question I got about this graph was as to why I placed fascism higher than communism. Well, although both systems are at the bottom and both are anti-freedom, the fascists are mostly overt about their oppression whereas communists are covert. As an example, the Nazis, who were fascists, had zero tolerance for people who had different viewpoints or if they even looked different than them. As such, they oppressed and killed millions in the process of trying to overwhelm others.

Unlike the fascists, who are overt about their wrongdoings, the socialists/communists speak of help while at the same time they are poisoning your mind and water well, all in the name of help.

Ironically, Hitler, the leader of the fascist party, was more of a communist (by the definition of communism above) and less of a fascist. He spoke of helping his people and of a greater future for Germany, while sending thousands of German citizens to be killed either in prison camps or in the battlefield daily even after he had realized that all was lost.

Here I am just making a technical correction since most people have it wrong about Hitler. I am beating no drum for fascism as it being any better, as they are both totalitarian systems and the antitheses of freedom.

Freedom

vs

Socialism

CHAPTER 1
HIERARCHY OF IMPORTANCES IN LIFE

As we look at the political and economic landscapes of different countries around the world we ponder as to what caused the state a country is in and want to know who and what is responsible for the outcome of things.

We ask questions such as: "What caused country X to be wealthy and why is country Y poor when both countries have equivalent resources?" Why are some people trying to leave their country and can't get fast enough to another? What is so special about country X versus their own? Said otherwise, what causes success and happiness in a society? Is it natural resources? The political system? Or is it due to innate differences amongst people?

All of the above is like asking, "What came first? The chicken or the egg?"

A lot of my friends who are scientists, believe that education and science are what is driving our world today and that it is the main cause of why one country is better off than another.

But who developed the educational system of the Country and on what philosophical basis? In regard to scientific research, why was Project X promoted and funded instead of Project Y?

Following are my beliefs about the hierarchy of life's systems and causation of outcomes:

First is the Philosophy or one's beliefs about life.

Then comes Politics

After that is Economics

Last is Science

Explained further:

1. A people's belief system or philosophy about life is what drives all their actions.
2. Based on these beliefs or philosophy, certain political ideas and a governing system come about.
3. This political system, which is established based on the people's philosophical beliefs, creates, promotes, and supports a certain economic system.
4. The politicians, social leaders and the economy makers, (merchants and industrialists), create, directly or indirectly, the educational system of the country. This of course is influenced by the philosophical beliefs of all the people in it. As such the exact type of education and the desired scientific projects are approved, promoted and financed. Thus, science is last in the hierarchy of things and it's based on the first three.

Notice that point #2 and #3 can interchange, especially if you look at it in terms of individual basis. Meaning, one's philosophy or beliefs about life, affects his/her economic state as well as what political system he supports.

To understand and appreciate the above hierarchy better, one needs to look at history in order to see the truth in it and how the philosophical beliefs of a people created their political and economic systems, which funded or did not fund, different educational projects and/or scientific research   The best example is during the medieval ages which is considered to be the time after the fall of the Roman Empire and before the Renaissance. During that era which lasted over 1,000 years, scientific research and science in general were halted and not promoted, as they were considered to be the works of the devil, **based on the philosophical beliefs of those times.**

As seen from the above then, it is the philosophy or the beliefs of a people about life and living that comes first in the hierarchy of importances and everything else follows, as will be explained further on the next pages.

Chapter 2

A PEOPLE'S BELIEFS ABOUT LIFE DETERMINE THEIR POLITICAL SYSTEMS

As seen from the previous pages, how people conduct their lives is directed and controlled by their overall philosophy and beliefs about life and living. In other words, whatever your philosophy and beliefs are, it is that which dictates your conduct with people around you and the actions you take in your life.

So, what are your core philosophical beliefs? Do you see a world with abundant resources or do you see a world of scarcity? Do you believe that people are spiritual beings, or do you think that they are meat bodies run by a ganglion of neurons? Are you an advocate of free enterprise and democracy or do you support totalitarian systems such as fascism or communism?

Whatever one's beliefs, it is what dictates how he conducts his life. Consequently, the sum total of the beliefs of a citizenry is the philosophy by which their country will be run on. These beliefs will be represented by the political system or political party if you will, which the majority of citizens will vote in power. In turn, this political party or system will govern and set the rules and laws for the entire country.

As mentioned previously: **The political system which a country is run on is the most important element which dictates a country's well-being in the present and for its future.**

If the political system of a country is that important then we as citizens must be extremely careful as to what system we promote and support.

At the top end of the political spectrum we have the free enterprise system, and at the other end we have the totalitarian systems such as fascism and communism. People have debated these two opposing concepts for years; but even the most fervent advocates or opponents of the two camps have never fully analyzed the difference of the two sides the way it is done in this book. In the following pages I will attempt to analyze the two sides in simple and basic terms for anyone to understand and fully duplicate their differences.

The differences of the two camps; Free Enterprise vs Communism and Fascism, or any other system which leads to totalitarianism are vast. **As such, the thought process and philosophy of the people who support free enterprise vs totalitarian systems is also very different.**

Since childhood, I observed that people do not see things the same way but, have vastly different viewpoints among each other. These differences come about from the people's different realities and understandings about the world, as I will present in the following chapter. These realities* are the data people use to formulate their overall philosophy about people and life in general.

*Someone's Reality = Whatever the person perceives to be real and factual for him. Reality for someone on any subject is what that person perceives it to be. The perceived reality might not be correct, but the person perceives it to be as such. If you try to tell one otherwise, you are suppressing him/her to some degree and therefore make him unhappy.

In the following chapters I will present several graphic depictions of some examples of possible realities people can have about themselves and others, their abilities, the economy and life in general. These graphic depictions show why two people can't possibly have the exact same reality or same understanding about things. So, let's take a look at the following chapters.

Chapter 3

DIFFERENT PERCEPTIONS AND REALITIES

WHICH CAN EXIST OR ONE CAN HAVE

ONES PERCEPTIONS AND THE DIFFERENT POSSIBLE REALITIES IN LIFE

ONE'S PERCECPTION	OBSERVED REALITY	UNKNOWNS
Percieved ability of a person by self and others	Observed Ability of a person	Unknown abilities of a person
Perception of one's worth to society by self and others	One's observed worth to society	A person's unknown worth to society
Perception of others regarding the Market	Observed behavior of a market	Unknown behavior of the market if xyz changes
Ideas people have regarding the needs of the market	Observed needs of the market	Unknown desires of a market
One's Perceived effects to society or economy if xyz changes	Actual behavior of the economy and society if xyz does change	Unknown behavior of the economy and people if xyz changes further
Perceived Facts about something	Observed Facts of anything	Unknown Facts about things

Shown on the previous page, are some of the different possible perceptions and realities people can have about themselves, others, society at large, the markets, or life in general.

As you can easily observe, there are many different possible realities which can exist in the world, of which no one can know <u>all</u>, no matter how powerful or resourceful one is.

I have witnessed and also read about, people who had vast power over others, such as, teachers, priests, kings, or presidents, in different totalitarian systems, who made very bad decisions which were detrimental to their people and it scared me. The fear did not come from the bad decisions these people made but from the fact that the people under them had no choices. The lack of choice and the arrogance of the omnipotent decision makers in these totalitarian systems made me realize that **people in high positions don't know all and/or don't care to observe better, especially if they have a monopolistic or tenure position**.

Of course, there are many other possible realities which can also exist, but **the examples in the previous page make the point of how it is impossible for one person, committee, or a group, to figure out all the different possibilities that exist or can exist about an economy or the people in it.**

Along these lines, a few years back a prestigious university conducted a study whereby they asked teachers to pick which of their students were most likely to succeed. This was to determine if teachers could really pick the future winners. The control group was: students picked at random by the researchers without knowing anything about them. The students were followed for many years after graduation. The results? It turned out that the students picked by the teachers were no more likely to succeed or fail than the control group which was picked at random. The conclusion of the study was that the teachers, who probably spent more time with their students than their parents, could not predict which of them would be the most successful in life. The reason? To begin with, the teachers were not able to really assess the true abilities of their students or shed off possible prejudices they had about them. Another factor was that the teachers could not predict the needs of a future economy or how each student's talents or shortcomings would best fit or not in that future economy.

For me, what the above study reiterates is what I have always observed: The fact that no one person or group will ever know all the different possible future conditions which can come about in life and people. Therefore, it's not fair for a committee, King, or a dictator in a Totalitarian system to pretend that it does and create havoc with people's lives by playing God.

If the above is true, then the entire idea of communism, fascism, or socialism is silly and very dangerous. It is certainly

not workable. Why would any one of us want one person or committee to decide our fate and the fate of others, when in truth, no one person or committee knows what each one of us is truly capable of, and certainly does not know what any market or economy, present or future, really needs or wants?

To make this concept more real, let's look at the plumbing trade as an example. Let's say that you are a plumber who just finished your schooling, got your plumbing license and are looking for a job.

In a true free enterprise system, the plumbing trade in your city would comprise of many different plumbing companies, which you can seek employment from. You could research each and find out where you best fit in to start your career. After you choose, and start out with an outfit, you stay on if you are treated well, but if you feel unappreciated or underpaid, you can seek employment with a different plumbing company or decide to start your own.

But, in a totalitarian system, such as in communism or fascism, there will only be one large government plumbing company controlled by a committee which will give you your job. The committee would be headed by a master plumber or politician (pencil pusher) who thinks he knows what is best for you as a plumber and as a person and also thinks that he can predict the city's future plumbing needs and wants. In this scenario, where all the plumbing services in the city are controlled by a committee, or "one boss", you would naturally feel very suppressed. This committee, or master plumber, who will oversee all plumbers in the city, cannot be fair to you, or to the other plumbers, since they cannot really know you or the market's plumbing needs or wants now or in the future. Nevertheless, they will decide for you, believing that they do know what is best for you, and think that they also understand the needs of the market, when in truth, they know neither.

By the way, there are committees in government who spend enormous amounts of taxpayer's dollars to study the needs and wants of the future job market. These are wasted dollars at best and for the most part provide misleading conclusions. Why? **Because there are just too many variables in life, with people and evolving technologies for anyone to be able to predict the future job market.** People who conduct these studies of course will always defend them, so that they can keep their jobs.

What one person or a committee thinks about the needs or wants of a market, or the capabilities of the people involved, could be far from the truth of what the market's real needs or desires are, or what people's actual abilities might be.

The above paragraph explains the reasons why the true free enterprise system and the freedom of choice it provides is best suited for the governance of people over any other system. **If allowed, "Mr. Market" will promote and reward the most desired and the best possible solutions for people and life in general.**

The above is possible, with a certain caveat of rules which you will see as you read the rest of the book.

On a personal note, early on in life I made the decision to own my own business and have control over my work and life in general. Reason? As I worked for other people, I realized that they could not see or did not want to see my talents or what I could do for the enterprise I was employed by. I felt, rightly or wrongly, that others would not appreciate the service or the products I was delivering and therefore would not reward me properly. True or false, that was my perception and therefore I have always been a proponent of the free enterprise system. It is the only system which provides people with the opportunity to prove themselves and allows them to express their creativity as it best suits them and rise or fall at their own volition.

Chapter 4

GRAPHIC DEPICTIONS OF FREE ENTERPRISE VS TOTALITARIAN SYSTEMS

What are the basic differences between True Free enterprise thinkers versus Communists or Fascists? They are the different beliefs, which each have about people and life in general.

a. The socialists or communists want to believe that all people have more or less equal abilities and desires and that if they do not, they ought to and therefore, they reason, it is moral and ethical to use the power of the state to make us all even, whatever this means to them.

b. The fascists like to think that they are superior and more right than others and therefore they think that it is moral and ethical to force their "right" beliefs on everyone else.

c. The true free enterprise thinkers are clear observers of life and understand that people are all different with vastly different abilities and desires. As such, they know that no one person is equal in ability or ambitions as another person, but we are all different in every respect and especially in our beliefs about life. Therefore, for any political system to be workable, it must take into consideration these differences among people, in its attempt to govern them properly and fairly. More on that in chapter 5.

Now let's take a look at several graphic depictions of the above thought processes which show how the socialists, communists and fascists look at people and the world in general as compared to the true free enterprise thinkers.

1. GRAPHIC DEPICTION OF THE SOCIALISTS AND COMMUNIST'S VIEWPOINT OF PEOPLE AND LIFE

The socialists and communists are trained to believe the following:

1. All people are born "even." Then opportunity and luck strike some of them who get into advantageous positions.

2. As these "lucky ones" get into a higher or advantageous position they cause others to feel inadequate.

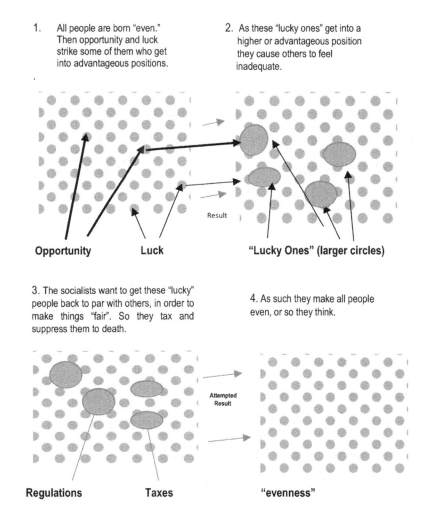

Opportunity   **Luck**   **"Lucky Ones" (larger circles)**

3. The socialists want to get these "lucky" people back to par with others, in order to make things "fair". So they tax and suppress them to death.

4. As such they make all people even, or so they think.

Regulations   **Taxes**   **"evenness"**

The circles in the sketches above represent the People in a society or country in general. The size of the circle represents the power and influence one possesses. The larger the size, the larger the power and influence.

45

2. THE BELIEFS OF A SOCIALIST OR COMMUNIST

The Communists are trained to think, not observe, that all people are born with roughly equal abilities, talents and desires. They are further indoctrinated to believe that man is a meat body, a vegetable or robot if you will, and not a spiritual being. These vegetable meat bodies or Pavlov's "dogs" (same difference) are only different, they reason, because they were "watered" differently or had better food or advantageous circumstances while growing up. According to Communistic belief, anything people do differently than others or any willingness to be more ambitious is an abnormality, which needs to be straightened out by their system. They further claim that any great success comes from luck and circumstances. As such they assert that those "lucky" or abnormal "ones", must share their luck with the rest of us regardless of how much more intelligently or harder they work. If they don't share, they must be punished because they are behaving in a very unkind or unfair manner. What about the argument of hard work or ambition or higher intelligence? The socialists claim this is due to luck, genetic or familial, therefore these "lucky" people, must share to make things fair. What if they don't share? Well then, they will force them to do so via high taxation or downright confiscation. But what if these "lucky" folks decide to leave the country and take all their talents and wealth with them? The communist reason that they should stop them from leaving or taking their wealth with them for the "benefit" of all. Ok then, what if they stay and decide not to work as hard or create as much? Well, they claim that they can force them to create and work just as hard, but that's a weak argument, as they really have no solution for that and therefore do not address this point very much.

Communists refuse to observe and cannot accept the vast differences among people. They cannot understand the vast contributions a small minority of citizenry (perhaps 1%), make toward the prosperity of any society. They erroneously believe, and this is probably their basic flaw, that what these talented few do, can be done by many other people under a communist regime. An incredibly flawed observation or should I say lack of observation.

Because the above is not true, as witnessed in all communist regimes throughout history, **communism creates psychotic people who lie about everything because they live in a system which is a total falsehood.**

The truth is, that despite all the feel-good speeches of the world's smooth talkers, people are "created" and born with vastly different talents and abilities. It is as if a playful God made us such, in order to create a game. A game called life and livingness.

By the way, people do better in life if they look at it as a game. Since they do better it means the concept of looking at life as a game works. If something works, it means it contains truth in it. Therefore, the concept of life as a game is true.

Most people in this game called "Life" want to do better and rise above their current state and not be cogs in a wheel. They wake up every morning and are eager to play the game. They will play this game well to the degree that they are allowed to play it freely and are rewarded for their efforts.

For something to be a game it must have excitement and the chances to win or lose if you don't play the game well. The game must also have freedom of choices. Communism takes out the chance of winning and offers no freedom of choices, therefore we have no excitement in it. As such, people in it feel that there is no point in playing this game. Therefore, a Communistic economy is constantly shrinking since there is little creation in it, due to lack of games and incentives. Nevertheless, it competes against other economies, which are constantly creating. It therefore falls behind, and its people end up living in misery. Imagine if only one US state was non-communistic while all others were; anyone with any talent and money would move into that state and the rest would starve.

The leaders of the Communists or socialists, as they are known today, know the above facts very well, and therefore

want to turn the entire world into one big socialistic/communistic state in order to mask the unworkability of their system and easily suppress the truths presented in this book. That is the reason behind the globalization movement going on in the western world today. They advocate such a system because, they claim, that capitalism a word which is purposely confused with free enterprise, creates greed and injustices amongst people. This greed and injustices get expunged, they claim, when communism comes to power. **Supposedly, all these greedy people become selfless, according to communists, as soon as they are exposed to their socialistic philosophy.** Otherwise said, a person will shed off any feelings of greed and will have no lapse of judgement as soon as he starts working for the government, be it a communistic or a fascistic one. I'm not sure how this makes any sense to anyone, but the socialists, fascists, or communists think it does.

In addition to the above flawed thought processes, **the communists also believe that the smart and able people will continue to work hard to feed the rest of us without any special rewards.** Well, that's a total lie, it will never happen. The smart and able people know that they are smarter and more able than others. Why on earth would they create great products or services by applying their God-given talents day and night without any special rewards than the guy who just sits around or spends his entire day at the beach? They will either figure a way to get around the system and make a lie out of socialism* as for example in Sweden or will simply not create anything beyond and above what others create, to the detriment of all.

*A lie out of socialism: Best example is Sweden, which is considered to be one of the most socialistic countries in the world. Well did you know that the financial disparity between the rich and poor is higher in Sweden than in any other country in the world except India? That's not very socialistic is it? Most people do not know that about the Swedish "Socialists". See the story about the Welemburgs in *The Economist (March 10, 2016 edition)*. The Welemburg family, probably the richest family in Sweden, at one point controlled 45% of the entire Swedish stock market. That's not very equalitarian is it?

In another example, a few years back, I read in an international publication that *Abba,* the Swedish popular singing group, had paid the most taxes in Sweden for that year than any other Swedish company. I wonder what these multi-billion-dollar Swedish conglomerates like Volvo, Saab etc. did with their earnings that year. (Wild stuff about these Socialists, Ha!)

Now let's look at a graphic depiction of **what REALLY happens under socialism, communism, or fascism.**

3. WHAT ACTUALLY HAPPENS UNDER COMMUNISM OR FASCISM

A COMMUNIST OR A FASCIST COUNTRY

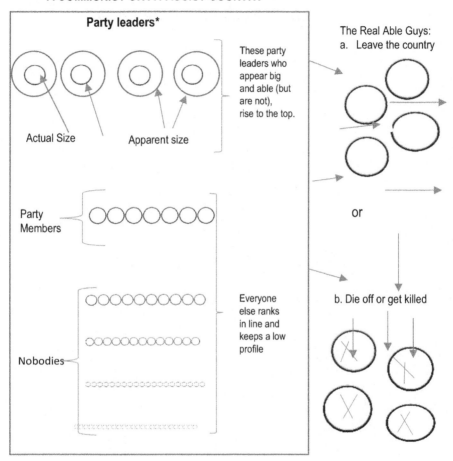

Party leaders*

These party leaders who appear big and able (but are not), rise to the top.

Actual Size   Apparent size

Party Members

Everyone else ranks in line and keeps a low profile

Nobodies

The Real Able Guys:
a. Leave the country

or

b. Die off or get killed

*Party leaders

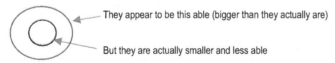

They appear to be this able (bigger than they actually are)

But they are actually smaller and less able

Now let's look at a graphic depiction of what happens in a TRUE FREE ENTERPRISE SYSTEM.

4. THE FREE ENTERPRISE VIEWPOINT

A free enterprise thinker is of the belief and opinion that people are born with different abilities, needs, and desires and therefore have different chances to succeed in life.

See sketch below:

People with unequal abilities throughout the world
an easily observable fact.

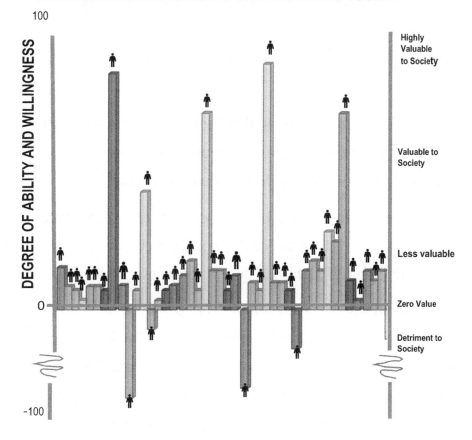

The above is another graphic depiction illustrating the differences amongst people in terms of abilities, willingness to produce and contribute to society **over a lifetime**. **Some people contribute greatly, others very little, if any, and some take away from society.** Because of these differences amongst people, we need a true free enterprise system to create a workable and therefore livable system which allows people to be able to function properly and consequently be happy, or at least happier than in any other system.

Why are humans so different? Well, that's a religious question and not for this book. The fact that we are different is an easily observable fact. It's as if a playful God or gods made us this way in order to have a game.

The question posed in this book is: "How do we create the most optimal society in terms of political and economic systems based on these differences among people?"

The free enterprise thinker knows that forcing people to be "even" or rewarding them all equally, regardless of contribution, is suppressing them to the highest degree and it never works.

What works is the attempt to bring about a plethora of teams, based on people's different desires and abilities, exchanging with each other as they see fit, in a true free enterprise democratic system creating through exchange and competition an ever increasing economic and technological pie. See next page.

A TRUE FREE ENTERPRISE SYSTEM

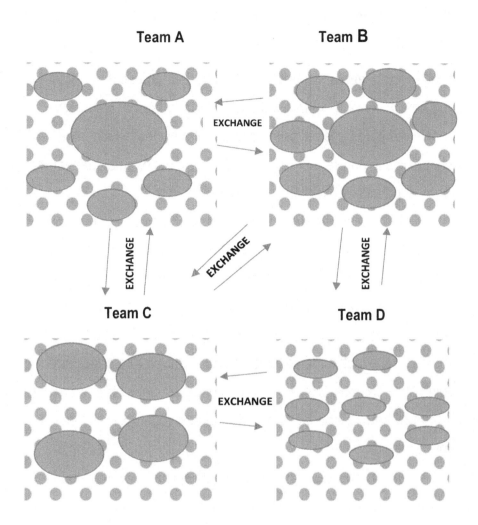

Different teams, with people of vastly different abilities with various configurations and matches. The arrows represent exchange of ideas products and services. **The team members have vast choices among teams since a true free-enterprise system has no monopolies or oligopolies in it.**

Here, I would like to strongly point out to the reader that the graphic depictions of the previous page is the essence of the entire book.

It fully depicts and describes what true free enterprise is all about and how it works. True free enterprise is not a system where rich people get pitted against poor people, but a system which takes what exists in nature and arranges it in the most optimal manner for the best possible governance of the people in it.

What I am asserting here is that due to the uneven nature of mankind, this is the only correct and therefore most workable system of governance that can possibly exist in any society.

I am very aware that this is a very strong assertion, but if you agree that people are uneven and different, you will most definitely come to the exact same conclusion and no other. The conclusion being that: The only workable system of governance among people, is many teams competing and exchanging in a democratic free enterprise.

As you can see from the graphic depictions presented in the previous pages, in a true free enterprise system, all teams have their differences and people can change teams as they wish, to better suit their talents, needs, and desires. In such a system, a **Janitor, has a very important post** in any company or organization. If he is not treated well or what he thinks is proper treatment, he has several other companies (options) to offer his valuable services to.

Each organization must treat its good janitors well, otherwise it will lose them to the competition. Also **the janitor of today can become the CEO of tomorrow and no one can label anyone as, "just a janitor".**

In a totalitarian system on the other hand, a janitor is labeled and ranked by the "omniscient" party leaders as a "**Janitor**" and is considered to be at the bottom of the totem pole of society and treated as such by the elites who determined that this person is, **"just a janitor."** In such a system he has no choice but to accept the treatment of a "janitor", whatever this means to the Elitists of such a system. It is the exact opposite of what the communists or socialists claim that happens with all their comrades. This concept is described well in the book *Animal Farm*, where it is proclaimed that although all animals are equal, some animals, are more "equal" than others.

Monopolies or oligopolies are considered to be the epitome of capitalism as they are confused with free enterprise. In truth, they are both close cousins to socialism. They can suppress people greatly by restricting choices and charging fees not supported by the market and or give poor service (since people have no choice) and therefore give a bad name to free enterprise. This consequently gives fodder to socialistic and polarizing ideas, as they create an us and them society. **As such, monopolies are the precursors of socialism and communism.**

57

Unions. How do unions come about? Are they justified? They are created due to Monopolies. If you allow monopolies and oligopolies, unions and socialism are inevitable and fully justifiable. It's the only means workers have to protect themselves. But Unions are also a form of monopoly and socialism all into one. There is only one Union (monopoly) and all people get paid almost equally give or take a few dollars (socialism). Unions reward the low producing members approximately as much as the high producers, and as such penalize those who are more productive than others. Long-term unions are a failure unless the entire world becomes a large union, or a communistic state, and then the politicians will control it.

In a true free enterprise system, unions are not necessary nor are they desirable since they stifle freedom of choice, creativity, and any effort above the norm.

A Very Important Note on the different abilities among people

I keep saying throughout this book that people are uneven and that we all have different abilities and desires. But notice that:

a. I do not specify who or what is better, or

b. That a superior judge should adjudicate who deserves what rewards.

The market will decide on all of the above.

The best example about this is the Bible story of David and Goliath. As the story goes, God gave David, a lowly shepherd boy, the ability to be good with the sling shot; to Goliath, a big and scary looking man, the ability to crush anyone and win. Who was better? What ability was more superior? Most people would think it was Goliath's, yet when the two competed, the "market" decided in favor of the sling shot and the lowly shepherd boy.

The above example best describes my viewpoint on this entire matter of "unevenness" which I refer to throughout this book. We all have different talents and abilities. As such, I believe we should be allowed to flourish and prosper by exhibiting these to the world; and not for a master to decide our place and level of prosperity in society.

Chapter 5

GOVERNING PEOPLE WITH

DIFFERENT REALITIES

Considering all the different realities, desires and needs which can exist among people, how can we devise a system for the most optimal governance? Otherwise asked, how do you allow for people to express their ideas and creativity and yet keep the governing political system and the economy on solid ground, since most people's ideas and realities do not pan out in the real-world economy?

The only way to accomplish this is by doing the following:

a. Allow people to express their ideas at their own risk, such as the freedom to start their own business or even their own political party.

b. Not interfering with beneficial ideas, systems and products and allow them to flourish, benefiting all of us in the process.

c. Permit non-working ideas and/or systems to fail, revealing to all what does not work and what is not desired by the market.

The only thing that accomplishes all the above is a free enterprise system with as little interference by the government as possible.

Don't get me wrong about government, I do not for one-minute think that we need no government, we do. But we need a government that enhances the above and not one that squashes them for the benefit of the bureaucrats. More on that in the following chapters.

An ideal political system would set up a government which does the following:

1. Protects the citizens' freedoms internally and externally.
2. **Helps its citizens to get the best possible education.**
3. Be a fair, and proper referee of the game of the economy.
4. Help **its citizens, create** the best possible economy for the country.

This should be the main role of government, and not micromanaging the economy or people at large.

The above is necessary because no single person or governing body can ever predict the future market or the many different possible realities and circumstances which can exist in the economy. Therefore, to allow a governing committee or a single individual to oversee and decide for all, as in communism or fascism, is suppressive and certainly not a workable system.

If you support socialism or communism, I ask: "Is it because you don't want to take responsibility for your life, hoping someone else will do it for you? Or is it because you never thought things through as above?

As mentioned in the previous pages, I advocate for a **True Free Enterprise system in a Responsible Democracy***.

It is the only system which takes the natural unevenness of the state of life and the unknowingness of the future to create the best possible results and happiness for the people in it.

*Responsible Democracy: A democratic system which gives greater voting power to citizens who take more responsibility for others and the country in general. From the book *What is Wrong with Democracy and How to Fix it.*

Chapter 6
THE MAKINGS OF AN ECONOMY

1. Definition of Economy

Since we are talking about the economy and how the political systems affect it, let's first define the word and see how it comes about in the first place.

The word *Economy* comes from two Greek words, *Ecos* and *Nomos*. *Ecos* means the house and more general the establishment of an area (houses). No*mos* means rule or law. So, the word economy refers to the rules about the house or the larger establishment of houses around us, which one can extrapolate to mean the rules or laws about our society in general.

Today we have further expanded the meaning of the word to be about the rules regarding business, money or finance. An argument can of course be made, that the rules about money and the handling of finance, affects the well-being of the people, their ecos (house) more than anything else. The layman has described this concept with phrases, such as: "Money talks, B.S. walks" or "it's all about the economy stupid", and the "Golden Rule", meaning: he who has the gold rules and or sets the rules, same difference.

The economy then, as the word is used today, is all about the handling of money, such as the growing, transferring, saving and the investment of it, individually and/or as a society at large, which includes governments.

2. The Creation of an Economy

Since we established that the economy is all about money and the financial well-being of the people in it, let us see how it comes about and what causes its growth or lack of it. In other words, how does an economy get created and sustained? What causes one country to be well off and another to be in poverty? What causes one company to be profitable and another to go bankrupt? Following are my thoughts on the subject, which at first glance will appear basic or primitive, but upon further observation it will be evident that these steps are not followed by most societies and/or the majority of companies.

An economy, or the making of money if you will, is created by at first **attracting attention via marketing and advertising**. You say, "Hey, we are over here, and we are developing a new shoe, a new computer or the same old thing but in better surroundings with better staff and therefore better service." You get the idea.

After marketing comes sales. The people come to your store, neighborhood, or country and you sell to them. The subtler and less pushy the sales, the better. The best sales techniques are the ones that get the customer to reach for the product on his own accord and then want even more.

After sales comes **the exchange of money** and **the delivery of the product or service**. You need to get the money and make sure you make a profit. **Without a profit any business endeavor is not fun, but more importantly it is not sustainable.**

The quality of the product does not necessarily need to be great, but it must work; and you need to make sure **the customer perceives that you are better** than the competition. If he does, you win. If he **does not**, even if your product is better, **you lose**.

As a general rule, your staff and customers do not care about you. All they care about is themselves. They instinctively think: **"What's in it for me?" You need to answer that better than the competition, in order for your staff and customers to stay with you.**

Therefore, good PR is critical. You must let more and more people know about you and the great things that your products and services do, so that you get more sales.

You keep repeating the above in the same order and your economy expands. Simple and basic!

But **what is the fuel** that makes the above scenario possible and keep it moving and expanding at a certain speed? It is a system or an infrastructure if you will, which becomes possible via **INCENTIVES!** As such:

**AN ECONOMY, ANY ECONOMY, IS CREATED BY INCENTIVES.
INCENTIVES IS WHAT DRIVES ALL, EVERYTHING ELSE IS
JUST A PRETENSE.**

In a book promotion lecture I gave in Athens recently, I asked my audience to tell me the reason Greece has such high unemployment. Afterall, Greece is a small country with many resources. Given the proper incentives they should constantly be short of labor. But that is not the case. So, I asked my audience as to the why of such high unemployment. My audience came up with all sorts of answers. But none of them were the real reason. So, I told them: "The real reason you have high unemployment here is because the current and prospective employers in Greece, do not have enough incentives to hire people." In fact, they are penalized by the socialist government in all sorts of ways for hiring and employing people. The Communists in Greece have been "educating" the workers for many, many years, that their employers, "their bosses" as they call them will always exploit them. As such they have convinced the people that the communist party would be a better boss for them, if they controlled the economy via the government instead of the entrepreneurs. To "prove" that, they push for suppressive regulations on everything and especially about employing people. So, I said to my audience: "**Ultimately employees become a burden and not a leverage for increased profits, therefore nobody wants to hire these burdens and**

69

therefore you have high unemployment." Consequently, these unemployed people look to government for help and therefore the government gets more support and becomes even bigger. In addition, **the socialist governments of Greece, via suppressive regulations and high taxation attempt to "prove" to the entrepreneurs that owning your own business, or your own real estate for that matter, is a burden, so don't bother, just get a job with the government or a monopoly, same difference.**

If you think the above applies to most governments and economies around the world then you get an A+ for observation.

As mentioned above, the most important thing for any economy to grow and sustain itself is to provide the proper incentives for humans to get out of bed every day and use their time and energy chasing opportunities and working hard at an endeavor.

The above paragraph is so simple it hurts, but most people do not get it and the socialists, communists or oligarchs, same difference, do not want them to get it.

Incentives don't have to be just about money. They can be about a higher position, the recognition of a job well done by the boss or the community or the appreciation of children toward their parents who take care of them etc. It could also be about getting the girl or the boy at the end. It can be about all these things and more, but **without incentives, people, and therefore the economy, do not move.**

Able and hard-working people will not offer their labor for free to any group or government regardless of circumstances. They will find a way to get around any government scheme, leave the country if they must or stop producing to the detriment of all. **This belief is shared by ALL HARD WORKING and CREATIVE PEOPLE**. If anyone else is telling you otherwise they are lying to you directly or indirectly. The above holds true today, it held true in the past and will hold true throughout eternity. This is so elementary that it defies logic as to why people don't want to accept it.

3. Protection of the Rewards and sustainability

What good will the rewards do for anyone if another can steal them via various routes including high taxation? **In order for the economy to be sustained and expand, there has to be a strong culture for protecting private property, investments, and savings.**

The socialists say that the rich need to pay more taxes. Well, I don't know what their definition of rich is, since they lump billionaires and monopolists with people who own small local businesses; but I can tell you what I think about taxes which is; if I get taxed no more than thirty percent of my overall take home income, which includes my house real estate taxes and the sales taxes on my personal consumption purchases; I am happy with the arrangement and I go on to create even more.

But if I am taxed higher than thirty percent of my total income, my interest wanes. If I am still creating, I will put a lot of my attention on how to reduce my tax liability, instead of putting all my attention on figuring out how to create better systems and expand my companies.

By the way have you heard the expression: The rich need to pay their fair share? Well, here is the breakdown of the tax burden as it relates to the different income brackets per the latest (2015) IRS Report on who pays what percent of taxes. The report reads as follows:

*"Upper-incomers carry the brunt of the income tax burden, IRS statistics show. **The top 1% of individual filers paid 39.04% of all federal income taxes in 2015,** the latest year IRS has analyzed. This top 1% reported 20.65% of the total adjusted gross income (AGI). Filers needed to have AGIs of at least $480,930 to qualify for the top 1% of earners*

***The highest 5% paid 59.58% of total income tax** and accounted for 36.07% of total AGI. Each filer in this group had AGI of $195,778 or more.*

The top 10%, those with AGIs of at least $138,031, bore 70.59% of the burden while bringing in 47.36% of individuals' total adjusted gross income for the year.

The bottom 50% of filers only paid 2.83% of the total federal income tax take. *Their share is so low because the figures don't include Social Security tax payments and because many of them got substantial relief through refundable tax credits."*

In other words, 50% of the people in our country, hardly pay any federal taxes, but they want the other 50% to pay even more than they already pay.

So, if the above is a fact, why is it that the politicians constantly harp on getting the top brackets to pay even more taxes? Because most people do not know these facts and the way our voting system is set up, I call it irresponsible democracy (see book ***What's Wrong with Democracy and How to Fix it***), it "pays" to bash the top 10% of the population to get the votes of the other 90%.

As you can see then, if you earn a lot of money you pay a disproportionate amount of taxes regardless of what the politicians claim. **The proper definition of taxes is: money confiscation by different government authorities.** What is the **most insidious**

from of money confiscation? It is via the printing of money out of thin air as central banks constantly do throughout the world.

Any printed money has no value regardless of what the government claims. **Real Money represents labor for actual products and services. The creation of money by a central bank, without the Real Money in the economy or extra gold backing it up, is equivalent to Monopoly money which is just engraved paper. It can only become valuable, by taking energy from the existing real money in the economy**. So what really happens is that, by government decree, this "printed" money is put in the system and it steals energy from the existing money in the economy. As such it **devalues any money people have in the bank or in their pockets.** Who has money? The savers...of course. So, money creation out of thin air devalues their money even more and consequently, they contribute an even higher percentage of taxes than it shows on the IRS records presented above.

Therefore, the top 1% end up contributing as much as 50% or more of the federal budget. If the socialists are successful in destroying this 1% then who will pay the taxes the government now gets from them? Also, who will employ all these people who are now being employed by the top 1%? The socialist will tell you that "The Government" will replace all these jobs. Yeah? And why has that not happened with all the socialistic and communistic experiments throughout history? Yes, they give people jobs, but they can't create any wealth. Thus went the Soviet Union, Venezuela, Greece, Argentina and many more.

I do agree with the phrase "people should pay their fair share", but not the way the socialists mean it, as you can see from the above.

What is the main problem with rich people in any society? There are just not enough of them.

4. Definition of Government

What is the definition of "The Government"? It's the people who are in charge of the civic offices. They, just like everyone else, have their own peculiar ideas about life and things. The people who use "The Government" as a noun are similar to the ones who use the word God as an all-encompassing power or father figure without defining its qualities or what it does. It's the type of thing which everyone defines as they wish at any particular moment. Therefore, the phrases: "it should be paid by the Government" or "The Government should cover XYZ service" reveals a complete misunderstanding of how the government works. **The government sells no products or services and therefore has no money of its own. It can only get money, always by force, from the ones who have money**. It can also create fake money, printed or credit, and force it to take energy from the real money* in the economy, another form of taxation. But, if there is no extra money to be confiscated, then the government collapses and a revolution starts.

*Real money is based on the production of desirable by the market, goods and/or services.

5. Freedom and Money

Money, in any form of good currencies or gold, is condensed energy.

For any action to take place around the universe it requires energy. Anything you do at any point in your life, also requires energy. Even moving your body around, requires energy in the form of food which you need to buy with money. To move from point A to point B also requires energy. As such, if you give $100 to a cab driver in Chicago, he will take you and your luggage from the airport to your hotel downtown and help you with your suitcases as well. If the $100 you gave him is fake and not real money, all action will stop, and he will NOT take you anywhere.

Anything that suppresses the ability of the people to have energy, is also suppressing their ability to be free. Since the most common source of energy on the planet today is money, **the best way to suppress people's freedoms, is via money.** No guns, no blood, no noise, just business.

Any system regardless of what it is called that reduces people's ability directly or indirectly to create and earn money is suppressing their freedom.

6. How do you Reward People?

There is a lot of hoopla and much to do about equal pay and pay based on education, seniority, gender, etc.

I can tell you exactly how I feel about paying people.

a. I will try to hire the best I can find for the job regardless of race, creed, or gender.

b. I will pay them based on what they do for my company and not based on race, creed, seniority, gender or degrees obtained by universities or any organization.

c. I will promote someone based on the ability to raise the statistics of his or her post and my company overall and could care less if this being is even from another planet and looks like a lizard.

I will do all the above ruthlessly, not because I like lizard people from other planets, but because if I don't, the competition in my town, country or another country will use their talent and beat me every time.

To summarize, I reward people based on what they do for my company and could care less about their race, creed, gender, or where they come from. Also, degrees do not impress

me, results do. I think this way because my customers don't care about me, but are looking to get the best possible service or product by whomever gives it to them.

7. The Free Enterprise Economy Abolishes Racism

A lot of times when people describe a subject, they usually use words which they do not fully understand and therefore don't get an exact agreement with others. For example, let's take the word "Racism". To date I have not found two people who agree on the definition of this word. The same is true for the words, "religion," "socialism", "communism", "capitalism" etc.

Racism to me, means discriminating against someone just on the basis of his/her skin color. This can happen in many different areas and endeavors in life if the discriminators have no repercussions. But in a true free enterprise economy racism is abolished. How you ask? Here is my argument: If a person of a particular race or culture offers you a service which is equal or better than another person's from a race "you prefer" and you don't hire him and not use his/her services, the competition in a true free enterprise system, will accept this person's service to your detriment. In addition, all people of all races have an economy, they consume stuff, produce stuff, and can demand support from the people who benefit from their economy and consumption in general. So, if you don't accommodate them, you will lose to the competition

78

who will accommodate these people and gain their support to your loss.

In a monopolistic society or big government (i.e. totalitarian system), people can be racists and create weird schemes, which are not supported by the market or common decency, and still get away with it. For example, if one controls the entire automobile market, he can hire people of his liking only, regardless of ability, and you will have no choice but to still get your car from his prejudicial company. Same goes for big government monopolies and all totalitarian systems.

The moral of the story is that, **in a true free enterprise economy, you better hire the best possible talent you can find, cater and be sensitive to your consumers' needs and wants regardless of race or creed, otherwise your competition will be sensitive to them and will run you out of business.**

The above is so true, I don't understand why people pretend that it is otherwise.

The ones who try to divide people using racism as an issue would make you feel that all conflicts and wars in history have come about due to racial differences and that socialism will abolish this evil from our society. But, if you look at history, you will discover that **all wars and conflicts in general, have come about due to different core philosophical beliefs among rivals and not due to**

79

racial issues. The Christian white Europeans have killed each other over philosophical differences more than any other peoples in history. They fought to promote Fascism, Communism, Democracy and religion. Religion as it relates to everyday life is a philosophical belief about life and livingness.

Different races and religions make earth a colorful and interesting place, no conflict there, but when your neighbor's core philosophy is very different than yours, regardless of race, or creed, there will be conflict. If your neighbor who might be of the same race as you, advocates that there can be consensual sex in regard to your children as early as age 14 or believes that it is okay to offer drugs to them, the two of you will have conflict. You get the idea.

It's ok and necessary to desire to have people around you who have the same core beliefs about life as you do, same ethos[1], but not ok to discriminate based on race. People who believe in a free enterprise system have a very different ethos than the people who advocate totalitarian systems and thus the conflict between the two. Some of my friends complimented me about these concepts, but I reminded them that this is not a terribly new idea. The ancient Greeks who were called Hellenes[2] (meaning the enlightened or the bright ones)

[1.]Ethos = The basic character or quality of a being

[2.] Hellene = from the word Helios = sun

claimed anyone could be a Hellene as long as he/she had Greek education and had the same core beliefs as the Greeks (same ethos) and not necessarily one born in Greece. The rest of the people they called Barbarians (people with different core beliefs) whom they had conflicts with.

8. Immigration and the Economy

Immigration is a hot topic around the world today. Citizens ask: "Do we open the borders more and if so, who do we let in?" Here are my thoughts on the subject.

We as sane people try to survive, and as such attempt to do better every day in order to increase our survival potential. Therefore, it behooves us to bring people to our country who will help us do better. For example, if we need more engineers, we should invite the best engineers from around the world who want to come to our country.

Most importantly though, **we want to allow people into our country who have the same core beliefs as we do. Their ethnicity or race is not important, but their core beliefs are.** If we as a country are composed mainly of free enterprise and democracy advocates, but allow communists in, then we will be injecting a deadly virus into our society. It's that simple. When I was submitting my paperwork to come to the United States at age 16, I had to sign papers attesting that I was not a member of any communist organization. I was very happy to sign such papers as I

81

felt that if Americans dislike Communism, I was coming to the right place, a country with the same core beliefs as mine.

Said otherwise, we want people in our country who admire our culture and want to emulate us and not the ones who disagree with our core beliefs. To fully understand this concept, watch the movie, "America America" by Elia Kazan. I can identify with the protagonist of that movie, who although found a much better life in Constantinople, decided to come to America, a country which represented individual freedom, justice, democracy, and free enterprise. Those are the very reasons I came to America and rejected the non-Hellenic ideas of modern socialistic Greece.

Ultimately, it is up to us as citizens to decide what we want. But, the more we open the borders, the less social nets, like: Social Security, Medicare, Medicaid, etc. we can have. The more social nets we desire, the more we need to control the borders. Therefore, we must decide what we wish to have as a country and act accordingly, but we can't pretend things are otherwise or that we can have it both ways.

9. Education in the Free Enterprise Economy

In order for free enterprise and democracy to succeed, it must have able citizens. The key to such ability is education, academic and life knowledge.

a. Education as it Relates to Government

One of the key functions of government is to make sure that its citizens get the best possible education. At the same time though, you don't want to make the government the main educator for the country. Instead, the government should be a referee and set academic (not social) standards for the school curriculum.

I am of the belief that **the government should give the money allotted for education to different private schools who will do the main job of teaching our children**. But, the government should test the students and consequently the schools on their academic performance. These private schools, in order to receive government money, will be required to educate all students from their district who apply to their school. The best schools will attract more students and therefore will get more money.

Have you heard how public schools in the inner cities are terrible and that minority kids get a bad education? Well, a privatization of the school system and choices for the inner-city students to go to any school they want would fix the problem overnight. The free enterprise system will come up with better, more effective teaching methods and the customers (the students and parents) will be the judge of that, not bureaucrats.

If a private school is great, it will attract more students who want to go there, and consequently the school will get more money and will be rewarded for its "greatness". If it's doing a poor job, less students will attend that school and it will be penalized as such.

No tenure for teachers, no unions, no concerns about keeping schools open in areas where it no longer makes any sense to have schools there. Also, no cumbersome school system to deal with, no politicians involved with it, just business. The business of teaching the students the basics of survival and ethics. Ethics being the optimal survival for self and others. Survival having to do with increased ability. The best ability each student can have. "Elementary", Holmes said.

b. **Money for schools**

The best way to finance the school system, and even academic research, is by the money printing (increase of the money supply) the government does periodically. My idea on this is as follows: As the economy grows the government will have to print more money to accommodate the increased business activity and increase the money supply, in the economy. This newly printed money should increase the money supply equal to the percent increase of GDP, (Gross Domestic Product...which is the cost of products and services delivered in the country each year), plus 1% or 2% more. See book *How to Fix any Economy in the World*. **Thus, the money, the central bank prints, for any reason, they call it quantitative easing, should be used to finance the entire**

school system and not be given to bankers as it is done now. You need to prop up the economy and want to print extra money? Well then do so, but give it to the schools to make people more able and they will solve any economy slump. This is revolutionary but simple.

Additional note: The students who test to be at the top 5% of their class should receive a 100% scholarship from the government (taxpayers), irrespective of their financial condition.

c. **Government and research**

The government should finance research especially the theoretical part of R & D in the school system and in the universities. Money should also come from a fee on all companies who want to access the data of that research.

The above concepts about the school system and education in general will do wonders for any economy and its citizens.

Chapter 7
COMPETITION AND THE
FREE ENTERPRISE SYSTEM

In a true free enterprise economy, no professions should have any special protection by the government except two subgroups, **surgeons** and **trial attorneys**. I want to guarantee a good living for surgeons so that they are not eager to cut people for money and I want trial attorneys to be busy enough, and therefore not hungry to take on frivolous cases, and clutter the system with dubious laws. Both of these subgroups should be viewed with reverence and their profession be treated as a public service and not as a money grabbing opportunity. **Everyone else except these two subgroups above should compete in a free enterprise democratic system for win-win exchanges and for the benefit of all.**

The main reasons totalitarian systems fail is the fact that its leaders do not realize the following two points:

A. **The market is the determining factor of any economy and not a committee of bureaucrats who put five year plans they deem desired and needed by the market five years from now.** That is one of the reasons the Soviet Union failed. Their "five-year plans" were laughed at by "Mr. Market".

B. **People who are allowed to pursue lifelong goals and create for their benefit, as in a true free enterprise system, will out create and out produce any totalitarian system by leaps and bounds, always!**

Let me give you an example about point A above, using the story of Facebook:

I consider myself a good businessperson and that I possess superior knowledge of economics, politics and social structures. Therefore, I could be someone the government would pick for one of these committees in a totalitarian state who put out those "five-year" future plans. As such, I would have listened to a young guy named Zuckerberg make his case about Facebook. Since I am "open minded", I would have allocated five or even ten million dollars for his team to experiment with this idea. But when he would have asserted that he needed more like one hundred million plus, in order to get Facebook off the ground and compete, I would have laughed at him saying: "Who cares about this silly social media thing? It does not seem to be that important as I see no great use for it. There can be several of these social media structures like your Facebook, but they will not affect the economy much anyway." I would have never given Mr. Zuckerberg a hundred million dollars to experiment with such an endeavor. Well, as you now know I (the "smart businessperson") would have been dead wrong. Why? Because, although for me Facebook seems like a waste of time "Mr. Market" had other ideas. Facebook today is a 500-billion-dollar company and I would have been completely wrong about it.

Again, the moral of the story is that no one will ever know what will happen in the market, one, two or many years from now, no one!

By the way if I was a powerful bureaucrat and had turned Mr. Zuckerberg down and another country got to build Facebook to the detriment of my country would I admit my error and be laughed at? Or would I have put someone in jail or worse, before he/she exposed me? Interesting thought process, right? Yeah, totalitarian systems and powerful bureaucrats are scary combinations, aren't they?

Today, Marx's capitalism, i.e. monopolies or oligopolies, interwoven with Socialism, have failed utterly across the globe. For proof look at governmental debt around the world. The debt is created by the promises the governments have made to their citizens and special subgroups, which they can't finance with the money they collect from taxes.

Unless you think that all this piling up of debt was all done purposely to enslave us all. Such inference would of course be at your own volition.

How do governments usually get out of debt and not confront their lies? War, of course! Look at history. So, socialism, the "equalitarian of all" brings war and death. Weird isn't it? Stay tuned on what happens as we progress into the future.

Although a lot of people would agree with the above, it is not easy to create and maintain a true free enterprise democratic system. The main reason being that the information contained in this book and other similar ones is not known to the majority of the people, and even to some angels as the following story proves.

An Angel's Story

It was the night before Christmas and Angels flew upon the world to perform miracles to honor this special day. As such this one young Angel appeared in front of a struggling farmer and said, "Behold my good man, in honor of this special night I am here to grant you a wish." The struggling farmer got scared and said nothing. The Angel then went on to explain that he was here to help him and if there was anything he wished, the Angel could do it for him. The farmer got a little courage and said, "Well my neighbor has a beautiful farm with much better soil than mine and plenty of water. My farm on the other hand, has rocky soil and my well has dried up so my animals are dying and I am sad.

The Angel at once, in a loud voice said: "IN THE NAME OF THE LORD!" then walked the struggling farmer to the window of his house. As he looked outside his window, the farmer could now see for the first time a spring in the middle of his farm with the water glittering in the moonlight. The entire farm was transformed with beautiful tilled soil, it was a sight to rejoice. The farmer started crying from joy and he and his wife could really see a bright future in this farm. They thanked the Angel, praised the Lord and ran out to take their animals to the spring since they were thirsty.

The Angel was happier than they were and moved on to another farmer who seemed to be struggling in a nearby village.

This farm was neglected and not well attended. The Angel found the farmer by his fireplace which was also neglected reading a book titled, "The Communist Manifesto." The Angel said, "Behold! In the name of the Lord and in honor of this special day I am here to grant you a wish. So, what can I do to help you this Christmas?" The farmer got startled but answered the Angel by saying: "Well my neighbor has a beautiful farm with lots of animals and is very productive. He acts so pompous at church and as he walks down the street, which makes me feel bad". So, the young Angel at once said: "Say no more, I understand your wish; you want to have a farm just like your neighbor, productive and with lots of animals." The farmer sheepishly responded: "Well, not exactly" at which point the Angel said, "Well then tell me exactly what you want, and it will be granted." The farmer continued, "I don't feel like working hard at this farm anymore, and what I wish is for my neighbor to sell off half of his animals because they are eating too much grass all around. Also, it is my belief that his farm should be more regulated by authorities so that we all know everything that he does for everyone's benefit."

The young Angel was taken aback and was speechless. He did not know what to make of this wish and it startled him to find out that there were people in this world who think this way. He wondered if the book the farmer was reading had something to do with this thought process. Nevertheless, this is data about people he did not have, and flew back to heaven to continue his education about humans as he realized it was incomplete.

Chapter 8

GREAT PROJECTS ⬅ GREAT AMBITIONS

Unlike Socialistic mediocrities which never created anything great, stellar **human achievements require great ambitions and massive doses of greed. Yes, greed and ambition in godly proportions.** Look at history and read about: Alexander the Great, The Roman Empire or the British Empire.

You cannot build a *Microsoft* or an *Apple* Empire without the desire from a Bill Gates, or a Steve Jobs wanting to be gods of a universe. They did not step out to make a buck or two for their families. They had ambitions beyond those of millions of people. **They desired to create their OWN UNIVERSE** such as the *"Microsoft"* or the *"Apple"* **universe.**

You can't build an empire without massive GREED and AMBITION that defy logic and the humble humanity of man. These big projects come about when humans want to be godlike. If you stifle ambitions and greed as in socialistic or communistic systems, you are also stifling advancement and growth in your economy and civilization in general.

As long as the "god" does not take the stuff with him when he dies, everyone benefits from his/her greed and ambition. To my knowledge no one has ever taken their empire or its wealth with him as he passed on, **so it is to our best interest to fuel the ambitions in all wannabe gods for the benefit of all of us.**

96

Karl Marx supposedly said: "To each according to his ability to each according to his needs." Yes, that works well if we are robots designed by a higher authority with a similar chip. But we are not robots but distinct and separate spiritual beings; therefore his ideas don't work. Each one of us is a god-like creature with the ability to think big and dream about conquering the universe. We also like to be free in the process.

The bureaucrats of a totalitarian state have an underestimation of the effort needed to reach a goal or to make anything worthwhile. It usually takes ten times more effort than one thinks it should. This is one of the main reasons socialism does not work, as a central authority cannot estimate what is needed or wanted and certainly cannot inspire individuals to bring forth the exceptional effort required. **Only driven people can put forth the effort demanded for the occasion and carry the day. They will do that, only if they are rewarded for their efforts and only if these rewards are protected by the State**. You say it is otherwise or you ask me to prove it. My proof that the free enterprise system works best is found in reading five thousand years of human history.

Anything that works has truth in it. The free enterprise, low taxation, democratic systems work and will continue to work, even if not applied perfectly and even if they get tainted over the years. **Athens, the city of the first free enterprise democracy**, no matter how rundown and tainted it got over the years, is still a great city even today with lots of ancient monuments and ample great literature tradition which inspires people throughout the ages. **Sparta, on the other hand, the world's first communist state, is just a prairie and there is nothing to see there**. The Spartans suppressed their people and gave nothing back to the world other than the destruction of Athens in the Peloponnesian Wars. The 300 in Thermopylae did not fight for freedom but died obeying the Rules of Sparta and especially the one that stated: "Take your shield, You Spartan Soldier and come back either victorious with the shield or dead on your shield, never come back defeated." They stayed and died in Thermopylae because they had no choice per the Spartan laws and not because they were taught to fight for freedom.

You say: "How about China, a more or less totalitarian state; look how great they are doing, they are becoming a superpower." Well the answer to this question is an entire other book, but let's just mention the following here. How many people do you know who are eager to move or are moving to China? The opposite is actually true, as wealthy Chinese try to move to Europe or America. Why do you think that is so, if they are so successful and winning?

By the way, how did China become so "successful"? Most people are not aware that China nets over 500 billion dollars each and every year from its "free trades" with America and Europe. Yes, China "outsells" the US and Europe by 500 billion dollars each from the so called "free trade". Does that sound like a conspiracy to build a country up and turn it to a "superpower", to the detriment of the Western World? Give me 500 billion dollars advantage each and every year, beyond and above what I buy from others and I will build you a superpower in a short time using a much smaller country than China. Let's stop propping up China and see what happens to them; the same thing that has happened to all totalitarian systems throughout history. It will implode.

What is the first thing that needs to happen to reverse the flow of capital to China or other countries? We need to stop chasing our companies out of the U.S. If you ask people as to why American companies left the country, they will tell you, it's due to cheap labor found abroad and capitalistic greed. Then I ask: "Why didn't the same thing happen after World War II?" During that time American companies did go to Europe where they found cheap labor, English speaking workers and countries that were more or less conquered and therefore directly controlled by the U.S. Yet, that was the best era for the American industry, inside and outside of the U.S. So the argument of cheap labor as the sole reason does not hold.

The main reason American companies left the U.S. in the 70's and early 80's was due to Unions, Governments (federal and local), and trial attorneys putting tremendous pressure on the industries in all areas of their endeavors. Same went for Europe, as their industries moved to other countries as well. As a consequence, Americans and Europeans were left without jobs. What was the solution to fix this destruction of the western world job market? It was a no confront of the problem by all parties involved. Instead of pointing out the real reason, which was socialism, and reverse course, they kept on the same line of action...more socialism; thus the companies kept going abroad. But these expatriated companies, now had another problem. Since Americans and Europeans no longer had good jobs, they could not buy their stuff coming from abroad. So all parties embarked on an easy solution, which was to: Print, and borrow a lot of money individually and as governments, so that Americans and Europeans would be "able" to buy the stuff these companies made elsewhere. As such we are in a debt mess with no end in sight. **The real solution would be to reverse course and be more business-friendly, i.e. create a true free enterprise system with a smaller government. Also to stop perpetrating the myth of free trade among countries. Free trade among countries is an oxymoron as you have no control over another country's laws over its population or the humane treatment of its labor force.**

What we should strive for is fair trade, not free trade. Meaning, you buy 100 million dollars worth of goods from me, I also import 100 million dollars worth of goods or services from you. This is a win-win deal, as opposed to free trade, open borders, win-lose deals. For more on that, see the book

Intelligence: Discover the 65 traits of Intelligence in the chapter Freedom Intelligences.

Unless of course, you think that the above was done purposely. If so, there would be no interest in solving this "problem". Such thought process would also be at your own volition.

By the way, I would not be against China or any other country becoming the new leader of the world as long as they have something better to offer than America does today. Totalitarianism is definitely not something better. **Totalitarian China, our biggest trading partner, suppresses religion on a massive scale. See Wikipedia: "Religion in China". Most people don't know this incredible fact. How is it that the majority of American and European religious groups have stayed quiet on this issue? Good question!**

Chapter 9

THE TWO NECESSARY RULES FOR
TRUE FREE ENTERPRISE TO EXIST

Unlike capitalism, true free enterprise is a balancing act between creating great wealth and advances in our culture yet maintaining a free enterprise democratic system. In order to do that we need the two necessary guiding rules explained below.

1. THE NO MORE THAN 20% RULE

Monopolies and oligopolies are closer to totalitarian systems than most people realize. No matter how benign their founders might have been, monopolies thwart competition and business freedom across the board. They become behemoths to the detriment of all. Due to their size and power they can influence our society in ways we cannot control. They can influence our elected officials and decide for us what to eat and what to take as medicine. They can provide mediocre services and/ or products without consequences. The biggest problem however is the prevention of competition and innovation from other competitive businesses. As an example, both North and South American continents have only had three automobile manufacturers to speak of for almost 100 years. How is this possible in such diverse and huge continents? It makes no sense. Two of them did a horrible job managing their affairs, went broke, filed for bankruptcy, and their customers, who got the mediocre product and service for all these years, were forced as taxpayers, to bail them out. Why? Because they were "too big to fail" they said. Okay, that is exactly what I am asserting here. **Never allow any company to become too big.** Problem solved!

Monopolies and oligopolies are everywhere. In the USA today, you better not go against the social media conglomerates as you practically have no other options. They can put anyone out of business at their whim. **How does this make any kind of sense, in a supposedly free enterprise economy with lots of antitrust laws on the books? It doesn't. How about the news media as they, are controlled by very few people?**

Along these lines, how can conglomerates be allowed to buy other conglomerates? Why is it to our benefit for a company that controls our food supply such as Monsanto, to be allowed to merge with a huge foreign drug company, Bayer? Is there no conflict of interest when the company that sells your food also sells your medicine? Think about it. I know most of you reading this were not aware of such a merger.

Congress constantly grills CEO's of monopolies or oligopolies about their wrong doings and attempts to "protect" us from them. Just recently Facebook's CEO Mr. Zuckerberg went on Capitol Hill to testify about a breach of users' data from Facebook. Both congress and Mr. Zuckerberg put up a show and looked good for themselves, but the public got nothing... just more of a monopoly. What's the solution? Split Facebook into different companies and create competition and let the public or customers decide which company they want to patronize or penalize. Anything else is not beneficial to the public, especially in the long run. We don't need Congress to protect us from the monopolies, we need a true free enterprise system which will fix these problems. We will protect ourselves using our ability to choose.

True Free Enterprise means two things:

a. **The ability for many people to be able to compete in any business endeavor.**

b. **For customers to have many choices.**

To accomplish the above we need the following rule which will work extremely well to guarantee a true free enterprise economic system, and therefore, freedom of choices. I call it the **"20% Rule"** which is:

No Single company or individual can own or control more than 20% of any market.

It works as follows: If a company becomes so big as to control over 20% of any sector of the economy the government tells its owners that they have one year to divest anything above 20%, otherwise the government will put for auction anything above 20% and charge 5-10% from the proceeds of the sale for its trouble to do so. Either way the owners will get paid for the sale of any portion over 20%, and it is okay if they get very wealthy, but **no one single**

company will be allowed to control more than 20% of any sector of the economy.

This rule could also apply for a state and/or a local economy depending of course on circumstances, restriction of choices for employees and customers, and overall benefit to the local economy.

A lot of people to whom I have explained this concept seem to have a problem with it, saying if someone deserves to be big why not let them? Well 20% of a large market sector like pharmaceuticals or automobile manufacturing is huge. **You don't want any company or individuals to control directly or indirectly anything above 20% of any market**. Such control is detrimental to free enterprise, democracy and individual freedom.

No matter how beneficial a behemoth might appear to be, it is always detrimental to our society's well-being at the end. **Regardless of how intelligent or hardworking someone is, he was able to develop this success based on a system supported by the rest of society. This free enterprise system needs to be preserved for future entrepreneurs.**

The concept described above is similar to **crossing the Rubicon River**, during the ancient Roman times. The *Rubi*con was a river in northern Italy. When Rome was a Republic and before it became an empire, if there was trouble in the North a general or two were given resources by the senate, to amass an army and go fight these enemies to protect Rome. But when the general was coming back from the expedition, he was to **dismantle his army before he crossed the Rubicon River.** To not do so he was considered a threat to the Roman Republic. Therefore it was treasonous if the general did not dismantle his army before crossing the "Rubicon".

Similarly, I suggest that **divesting anything above 20% is like dismantling the troops before crossing the "Rubicon" (the oligopoly or monopoly status).** It is a rule which will serve our free enterprise and democratic system well in more ways than people think.

This 20% Rule will have to include the public sector as well. No one person or one group should control more than 20% of the medical facilities, the school system, utilities, etc. Even the military should be broken in 20% units or less. The different branches will coordinate of course but the personnel in each unit should be off limits from the other branches and should be allowed to move to another military branch if they choose to do so. In other words, you can leave the army and join the navy if you so desire and are accepted by them.

I am no military expert, nor do I know all the workings of the military, but I know that choices and the removal of limitations do wonders for the human spirit. **People expand and become the best they can possibly be only when they have choices and freedom. This expansion can be so great and beyond anyone's**

expectations and create a society of incredible ability with a high standard of living for all. We just need to let it happen.

That is what made Athens, the founding state of democracy, very unique and the destination center of the ancient world...freedom and choices. It's this same allowance of expression of freedom of the human spirit which also made America the destination center of the modern world.

I have traveled to over twenty different countries on four different continents and what I have noticed is that the closer the country is to free enterprise and democracy the more well off its people are and more importantly, the happier they are. If you have also traveled around the world, you will agree with the above statement.

2. THE TEN PERCENT RULE

I am a very strong proponent of free enterprise and competition, but I also realize that in any society despite the best efforts of its leaders and educators, there is a percentage of people who never seem to be able to do very well. Why you ask? That's a long story and another study but we are dealing in facts. This percentage could be as high as 30% of the people in some areas. The reasons are many, but these percentages are there, and these people are constantly needing help to survive, no matter the best intentions of the rest of us. So how do you deal with that sector of our society?

My suggestion is to allow a certain percentage of tax money or resources for this population in order to help them become more able and also to keep the peace. But:

1. **The percentage needs to be FIXED at, something like 10% and no more, regardless of circumstances, otherwise you encourage people to be less and not more**.

2. The people in need of government assistance must not get the same political benefits as the rest who pay for them. See more about that in the book *What is wrong with Democracy and how to fix it.*

3. Every effort needs to be made to help these people to get off the assistance.

4. The churches need to play a bigger role in helping these people.

5. Goal orientated education in all areas of life and the attainment of a trade or profession must also play a key role in the effort to raise people out of poverty.

6. Any person able to work, should be given a job, no exceptions. There are all sorts of jobs people can do to help; cleaning the roads, planting trees, painting bridges, and much more.

7. Minimum wage should be reconsidered for special groups of people. See the book *Intelligence: Discover the 65 Traits of Intelligence.*

If I was to condense the above seven suggestions it would be as follows:

Help the people who can't make it become more able and make it. Any type of help should be staticized and therefore monitored for effectiveness.

I know very few people if any, who can't do something to exchange with others. We can all help and do something. Giving money to people just because, without an exchange, is degrading and encourages them to be less.

Chapter 10

WHY IS SOCIALISM SO APPEALING?

Life on planet Earth is hard and fragile. You get infected by a little bug and you die. Too hot or too cold and you are a goner. Today you have a good job and you are happy, tomorrow you lose it and you are miserable. People know there is cause and effect. They also know that the elements can be at cause and they at effect. They attempt to be cause over the elements, but they get beaten up either from the environment or people who are in charge and who don't seem to be doing a good job at running things. As such, many people can't get ahead but don't know the reason. Therefore, they are looking for leaders who can provide them with answers and will follow anyone who asserts to know.

All this amounts to, is that people can become easy prey to fat words and easy promises. That is where socialism comes in and wreaks havoc with humanity. Elitists who have great power and want to control others, use socialism as a tool to accomplish such. They preach that they will reward us all equally and much better then we are rewarded at present. Most people love to hear that, regardless of any truth in it. These elitists tell people that a system can force others to take care of them despite contribution on their part or special rewards for the contributors; a hysterically stupid computation and a total lie as this has never happened in the entire history of the world. They also claim that there is money everywhere which they can tax (confiscate) and give to people as soon as they come to power. The fact that this has not

114

happened throughout all socialistic takeovers does not stop the socialist candidates from promising such.

The real truth about wealth is that it's created by incentives. Once the incentives stop, then the creation of wealth stops and the entire country goes down and people actually get less not more. See Argentina and Greece as recent examples. After they sell people on the idea of socialism, they proclaim that the socialistic system comes from the hardworking people of the land and its an equalizer.

These are the horrific lies of communism and fascism. The end result? Fanatic people who support Totalitarian systems to the detriment of society and the human spirit.

Elitists in power do know that communism, socialism, or fascism, produces slaves and that is why they promote such systems. It's for their own goals of control and not the people's benefit.

The only workable governing system that we can have, considering the unevenness of humanity and the instincts of self-preservation and self-promulgation is a true free enterprise system with competition among many different teams in a democratic society. The smart and hardworking people among us will never work to take care of others at gun point and without incentives.

What this means to you, is that you constantly need to work on being more able and increase your exchange with society, instead of hoping that others will be forced to take care

of you, as is proclaimed by the socialists, communists or the like. It will never happen regardless of what they promise. The opposite is actually true. **The freer and more democratic a society is, the wealthier the people are and the more they care for and help others.**

The above is an honest observation as is this entire book, which causes more good than harm and puts order in a difficult world for the benefit of most and creates progress not regression. Proof? Again, look at history.

Not to get too philosophical, but the basic reason for accepting or believing communistic ideas is based on the belief that man is and was an accident of the cosmos i.e., the physical universe. It is the acceptance of the theory that man came from mud and from the shaking up of amino acids. This theory is very well accepted without proof, but with a lot of conjecture. Following is an article my son Constantine wrote for one of his school papers in college which rebuts the theory that "our universe and man came from an accident rather than intelligent design."

It's up to you to decide if you agree or disagree with the paper's premises but it's an interesting viewpoint and it relates to governing mankind.

AN OBSERVATION ABOUT THE IDEA THAT THE PHYSICAL UNIVERSE'S CHAOS, PRODUCED LIFE

Author: Constantine Alemis

To exist anywhere in space requires an original cause of some sort. The placement of your shoes at the front door was caused by you. The position of your car in your garage was also caused by you. The falling of the apple on the ground was caused by gravity. The movement and spin of the earth was originally created by some cause (collision, gravity, or even just designed to be so). **Therefore, it is an observable fact that there is a cause behind the existence of everything.**

Based on the law of inertia, for something to be in motion there must have been an original force that acted upon it. Following this original force, you can have a cascade of different causes because that new object in motion is capable of being a cause point to create effects on other objects. For example, if an asteroid was forced into motion, it can hit another 6 smaller asteroids which fly in different directions hitting another set of asteroids and this can continue until the end of time. This is a simple and true idea, but we should be questioning the motion of the first asteroid. How did it get in motion? What was the original force that acted upon it and by what means?

Many theories that trust in chaos to form the precision of our

117

universe, assert that this cause was the explosion from a densely packed mass at the beginning of time. This means that any object currently in motion is a result of that very first explosion permeating throughout the universe. Say this is true, then it must be true that **the only original cause that created this universe was the energy stored in that so called "singularity."**

However, the proponents of this theory claim this chaotic explosion produced a creature known as a human. **Somehow, the original and ONLY cause throughout the universe which was that first explosion produced a conscious being that is now in and of itself a cause point**; which can generate its own effects with its own self-determinism separate from that original bang. **This created cause point, i.e. mankind, can even counteract or reverse effects from that original explosion**. As man will develop the technology to blow up planets, create planets, stop earth's spin, or place force on some asteroid and generate its own cascades throughout the universe. This then means that man, is cause on the physical universe that supposedly created him. As such, mankind controls, manipulates, and instills order in a physical universe which specializes in chaos, and can create its own explosions and chaos. **We are now becoming the rulers of this universe and we can actually create effects separate from that original explosion.**

But this does not add up. An explosion of matter (cause) created a purposeless and mindless thrust of particles at high

speeds (effect) throughout open space which supposedly created, by an impossible chance, a conscious being who instills order into the environment and is becoming cause over the matter that supposedly created it in the first place. But matter, as we all know, has no volition of any kind. It has no mind if you will, it just exists.

Many theorists of course say that it just somehow happened, and we should be thankful the chaos lined up so perfectly to create us thinking entities. However, they have overlooked this single fact mentioned above, that: **mankind and life in general act as the result of a separate cause point, distinguishable from that original explosion of matter.** *Its purpose appears to be reproduction, survival, and replication which is a cause in and of itself.*

Therefore, we can observe that a causative entity or entities have placed their control over matter and instilled a purpose into it. *This can be a spiritual being, a god, or some cause point that generates its own energy.*

Despite the theorists the above is plainly clear to many people because they understand it innately. If for instance you show someone a book and ask if the book was created by chaos and random events, 10/10 will reply with "of course not." They know that someone thought through the design, the contents of the book, the creation of the pages, including its binding. However, it is much more likely for a simple book with words and paper to be created from this explosive big bang than is life itself. As such, if you found a book on a distant planet you would immediately know that life had been there, and you could not possibly think that this planet's trees clashed together perfectly and generated a meaningful book.

Chaos is not a rational or logical agent to explain the phenomena of life and the design of our universe, galaxy, or solar system. **Explosions are purposeless causes that create purposeless effects. Precise effects, precise life forms, aesthetics, beauty, and consciousness, are the result of a purposeful cause which knowingly is creating these things.**

All one has to do is to perceive one's environment and create ideas within the realms of one's own mind to observe awareness or consciousness. You are alive with purpose and ability. You know innately that you did not come from a purposeless explosion and the mud of this planet as demonstrated by the book example above. You can also observe that the physical universe is a destroyer and an agent of chaos. The universe's laws degrade the house you built, spoil your food, blow up stars, and kill off life. **If left alone even for an infinite amount of time, this chaotic and destructive universe would never produce life because it is simply not built into the laws of this physical universe for life forms to be created.**

In fact, even the physical universe is not as chaotic as we

like to think. It's far more organized than would happen by chance. Look at its basic architecture. There is a heavy body in the middle, be it a proton, a star or a black hole and it holds around it via gravity and centripetal force the entire physical universe "pieces", small or large. The atom has a proton holding electrons in place, the star has the planets around it holding them in place and a black hole is holding an entire galaxy and preventing it from coming apart. **Same architecture, same design, same concept for all physical matter large or tiny. Do you think that could be possible with two pieces of rocks smashing together or by a large explosion hurling matter into space? I don't think so.**

Along those lines, what do you think of DNA, and its ability to create a body? Do you think all that sequence came about from amino acids hitting each other over billions of years to develop this sophisticated bodies to be run by humans and all the other life forms? **It seems to me that life forms are designed and used by spiritual beings and supreme beings to propagate themselves throughout a planet with the purpose to survive and play a game.**

Many argue with the above thought process because they believe anything nonphysical such as a spiritual being cannot be proven to exist. To this I say that their observation skills are low, for the mere fact that any time one is generating a thought or idea he/she is partaking in a nonphysical activity. A neuroscientist of course will tell you that when you have a thought such and such neurons are firing in your prefrontal cortex which correspond to it. Well, let's assume that this is the case and those neurons are indeed the neurons corresponding to your thoughts. Let us also assume that the contents of your thought was a sunny day with a dog running in the yard and the smell of flowers hitting your nose. But, analyzing those neurons that were responsible for this thought will be disappointing to say the least. You will see a bland of ions composed of sodium, potassium and calcium, as well as amino acids, proteins and electrical impulses that resemble nothing of the thought you had. But there is, a nonphysical entity of this "picture" or "scene" you created with the dog in the yard. You saw the scene, you felt it, you even smelled flowers that were not present, but where is it? If you saw it before (from memory) and believe that all existence is physical, then you must be able to pull this "scene" out of your brain and see it in physical form via the neurons. We all know that this is not possible. So, is this scene a non-physical entity? Well, **since it is impossible for anyone to actually see the contents of your thoughts, by looking at your brain or neurons, then it stands to reason that the mental image, and that which created it, you, would have to be non-physical entity as well.**

The ability to create thought is pertinent to the discussion about cause and effect because thoughts are causes and are characteristics of consciousness; explosions and collisions produce

122

neither.

These data are, merely a collection of observations that anyone can do. **As such, I am tired of being told that explosions and chaos created beings with consciousness, ideas, emotions, and the ability to create effects, over the physical universe***.*

Many people have ideas based on data that is forced upon them. These "stuck" ideas crumble in the face of observation if they are not true. So, observe the world for yourself to find truths that make sense to you based on what you perceive and not what they tell you that you should perceive. Allowing data to be forced on you causes you to live life through the eyes and observations of another whose observational capacity may be lacking. Trust in your own observation and accept as true those things that hold up to be true only after you have observed them yourself.

Socialism Indoctrinates People to Look Down, Not Up

When one is down and out, he is apt to accept any kind of help whether from the good guys or the bad guys. But remember, the reason mice get caught is because they never ask and therefore never find out why the cheese is offered for free.

The socialists can give us all the free cheese they can confiscate from whoever today, but what will happen tomorrow when all the top producers stop producing, scatter, or get killed? Ask the

Venezuelans, Greeks, Argentinians, and most people from other countries around the world. They can fill you in on it and it isn't a pretty picture.

Socialism educates people on "the fact" that they are animals and what is needed is social engineering to corral these beasts as they are "evolving". But people are not animals and therefore are not happy when treated as such. They are spiritual beings, aspiring for something higher than themselves and an animalistic existence. What makes people really happy, is when they reach for the ethereal as opposed to the mundane.

The most aware among us want to reach for the stars and plan for the millennia for their team and mankind, as opposed to planning for say "retirement." Retirement planning does not get people excited, only grand future plans for themselves and their team they find exhilarating. Why you ask? It's because people innately know they are more than just bodies and as such they get excited about the future, not the present or the past. Creation and futures are exhilarating to people, restrictions and high taxation are not.

In Ronald Reagan's words: **"Socialists" ignore the side of man that is the spirit. They can provide for shelter, fill your belly with bacon and beans, treat you when you're ill; all the things guaranteed to a prisoner or a slave. They don't understand that we also dream."**

Chapter 11

IT'S NOT ABOUT THE PEOPLE

IT'S ABOUT WHO WILL BE BOSS

Another title for this book could be, **"The battle for control of the people and resources between the entrepreneurs and government bureaucrats."** This is what the battle between free enterprise vs totalitarian systems is really all about.

When it comes to governing a particular society or people in general, there are leaders or bosses who organize and run things. So, the question becomes: Who will be the boss or the leader of the people? Said otherwise, who will decide the fate of others and have control over their actions and destiny? This is what this conflict is all really about and not about free enterprise versus socialism. **IT'S ABOUT WHO WILL BE THE BOSS.**

This reminds me of a joke titled "Who will be the body's boss". The story goes as follows: When the body was developed, the different body parts held a conference to decide who will be the body's boss. After much arguing most body parts conceded to the heart and the brain, except the sphincter or asshole. He insisted that he should be the boss and when the other body parts started laughing at the idea, he got very angry. He got so mad that he tightened up so hard whereby nothing would go through, resulting in a very jaundiced body and a poisoned system. After a while, all the body parts were getting suffocated, so they stopped laughing and conceded control to the asshole as they realized that he had the ability to kill everyone including himself if they did not recognize him as the boss of the body.

The above joke plays out the same in every society, as you have the struggle as to who will be the boss of the people. Will it be the employers who provide jobs for them, or the politicians who can control both the employers and the workers using the laws?

In a free enterprise system, the entrepreneurs control the resources of the country and are responsible for the well-being of the people, their employees, at their own risk. In big government totalitarian states, the politicians or bureaucrats attempt to control the resources and the people of the country on the backs of the employers without any personal risk.

As a citizen of a country, do you want a system, where the most able control the resources and jobs in the economy and if they don't do well, they pass the baton to a more able entrepreneur? Or do you prefer a totalitarian one such as communism or fascism whereby the resources, jobs and your fate are controlled by tenured bureaucrats who most of the time have no proven track record in the field they are assigned to control? In a totalitarian system you have no freedom to change jobs and you are required to do as you are told by people of questionable ability and without any personal risk on their part.

By the way, when a government gets big, in order to sustain itself, it becomes the adversary of entrepreneurs by doing the following:

a. It takes away more resources from the free enterprise system and from the most able people via higher taxes. As such, in America today, see previous pages, over 50% of all federal obligations are paid by the top 1% of income earners, the entrepreneurs.

b. It asserts itself as boss over the enterprises and passes all sorts of rules and regulations which hinder production and/or the creation of better systems.

c. It also asserts itself as the workers' protector, and therefore their boss, by passing laws for the "protection" of employees regardless of proven necessity.

Since the majority of people do not **own a medium size business or real estate, they think the above does not apply to them, but it does. It applies to everyone, since whatever affects the top 1%, affects everyone else and vice versa. It's an interconnected economy** if the entrepreneurs of a country are not faring well, they will not be motivated to create, and therefore no one else will do well, as there will be no jobs for the rest of us.

In Greece, the socialists passed all sorts of laws to "help" the workers. The workers were ecstatic to get all these benefits from their employers, enforced by the government, until a few years later when they discovered that these benefits were not sustainable, and the businesses suffered and as such socialist Greece clocked the highest unemployment in the western world. Today, Greek workers on average make less than they did ten years ago and with much fewer benefits.

My take on all this is as follows. **BOSS = Responsible for others**. I want the one I designate as my boss to take responsibility for me and my family. If he/she gives me a job then to a degree I will allow him/her to be my boss. But if someone forces me to accept him as my boss but provides no opportunities for me and/or my family, then I refuse to allow this person any authority over me. Another way to answer the question of whom I will allow to be my boss is by asking: Will I be better off with this person being my boss, someone else, or no one?

Therefore, **"The Boss"** should be the guy or girl who takes full responsibility for the people under him and then leads them to the best possible destination for the time. Also, he should have a vested interest in the people's success and be penalized at least as much as the people under him if they fail by following his/her leadership or advice for that matter. In other words, the politician, business leader, or high priest, cannot keep enjoying the fruits of his/her position if the people under his leadership are going down and not up.

I can write an entire book on this, but if you reread and fully understand the above paragraph, you will figure out exactly whom you will accept as your boss.

HIGH TAXES

High taxation is the tool the government bureaucrats use to direct resources their way, so they can be the boss. This crushes the economy, but they don't care about that, what they want is to be the boss. In fact, the worse the economy the more important the bureaucrats or government become, as poor people always reach for government help.

V.A.T. TAXATION

V.A.T. stands for: value added taxes; meaning the government puts higher taxes on items which are considered unhealthy or unnecessary such as cigarettes or luxury items like yachts. In other words, non-vital items. Well, that's how it got started anyway and people accepted it. But remember since it's about who would be boss, the more taxes the better for the politicians, or so they think. The V.A.T. in Europe, which is now added to all purchased items and services, is more than 20% in some countries. This tax is collected up front, as a sales or a transaction tax. But the overwhelming majority of businesses around the world have profit margins of less than 20%. Walmart's profit margin for example is close to 4%. So, under such a tax system, which is the norm in Europe, the government will pre-collect from the entrepreneurs, the guys and girls who work day and night to create and maintain the business, more money than they can possibly expect to ever make via any profit. Wow! That's a lot of "incentive" for an entrepreneur who consequently thinks: "I can't wait to go out and work my guts off in order to collect 20% for the government in the hopes that I get 4% for myself."

Also, what do you think happens when the government takes 20% from each economic transaction and siphons all this money from the local economy? Do you think it slows the local economy some? Of course, it does, it kills it. But again it's not about the welfare of citizens it's about who will be the boss.

The funniest thing to me about this high V.A.T., sales or transaction tax, whatever you want to call it, is the fact that people don't understand it, nor do they understand how it kills their business and the economy at large. They reason: "I will sell my product for what I need to make, the V.A.T. will be paid by the customer not me, so it does not affect me". And that's the part I find funny, because people who say that, can't do a simple reasoning which is: If your product or service costs say $100, a 25% V.A.T. tax would take it up to $125 total. So, your customer, since he must pay the 25% tax for each item, $25 in this case, will only buy four items from you in our scenario above as opposed to five, if the V.A.T. was not there. **So, you will sell less products and services just because of this V.A.T. tax.** In addition, you must comply with all sorts of regulations, which are time consuming, costly and could be detrimental to you if not done properly, on time and by the right accountants. **All this amounts to, is less incentives for you to create.**

Most importantly, as mentioned above, the V.A.T. money leaves the local economy and only God knows where it goes. Very soon there is no money left in the local economy since 25% + 25% + 25% from each transaction, has fled the local economy and it went to the bureaucrats in the government. But, no worries, the bureaucrats, the wannabe bosses, will bring money back to the local economy by financing their cronies and their own pet projects, called governments subsidies, which **they perceive are needed for the country, their system or their party.**

The fact that most people cannot follow the above simple logic, I find terrifying.

A MODERN FORM OF TAXATION

Today the words: taxes, communism and fascism have gotten a bad name. Therefore, the politicians cannot promote any of these openly, and if they intend to implement any of them, they must do so in a covert manner, such as calling them by another name. Hitler called his fascist party the German Socialist Party. Most communist regimes call themselves democracies.

But how about more taxes? How do you get around that concept? One way is the V.A.T., or sales tax, which some people think, I don't know why, that it is not an income tax. But many others do see it as a tax and get upset about it. So how do the politicians who are trying to get votes by promising free stuff to everyone get around the raising of taxes openly?

Print money! Of course! Print "money" out of thin air. This way the government gets the money they need "without" openly taxing anyone and voila, problem solved. The government sends this printed paper to go out and get energy from the real money in the economy. As such, it drains energy from the people who have money. The public does not understand this and thinks that the printing of money does not cost them anything. The ones who get the free stuff of course do not care how they came about, they are just happy they got it.

This printing of "money", sorry, I meant the paper which the government forces in the economy to seek energy from real money, **is the most insidious form of taxation.** Since most cannot follow the above, the politicians get away with this new form of taxation which is totally masked. As such, people will work harder and harder and find that, regardless of how hard they work, they will not be able to get ahead. In fact, some working people will discover, that they will not be much ahead from the nonworking people.

This is insidious communism. No armies, no revolutions and no wars are needed. The politicians can just print money and create a totalitarian system where people think they are free. This is called dystopia in its fullest sense.

TAXES AND PRODUCTIVITY

If I had to design a tax system as to how to collect taxes for the government, it would be as follows:

Tax every transaction in the country at 20%. To be distributed as follows: 10% to the federal government, 5% to the state, and 5% to the local government (municipality, city, or village).

Finance a private school system and research, via money printing, mentioned and explained earlier.

The defense budget would come from taxing all property in the country between 1-2% of its value.

No other taxes or accounting needed.

The above will cause an incredible surge in productivity, freedom, and happiness among the people in the country.

THE SHAMING OF THE TOP PRODUCERS

The socialists constantly bad mouth and give false reports about the top 5%-10% of the most successful citizens. They say things about them, such as: "They don't pay their fair share", when in fact they pay far more, or that "They are unfairly privileged" because of XYZ reasons and other derogatory remarks. As such, they have created a negative feeling toward these top producers in the minds of the rest of the public. In fact, we are now at the point where even those top producers have accepted some of these false accusations about themselves as truth. Well, that is silly.

The top producers in any society are so valuable to the economy and social structure of their country that they should be rewarded handsomely; such as being able to be financially independent after several decades of creation and hard work. Yet most of these people are not financially independent even after 40 years of 7 day work weeks. Why is that? It is because of taxes, regulations, lawsuits, and even more taxes. In some countries, these people are even denied their pension which they paid in, over many years of hard work, because their government claims they already have "too much money" (see Australia).

As an economy is made up of incentives, if you penalize your top producers, then you will get less production from them and therefore shrink your economy to the detriment of all. For such examples, see socialistic and communistic countries throughout the world.

WESTERN WORLD'S BIGGEST EXPERIMENT

The west (meaning Europe and the U.S.), and the world they influence, such as Japan, Australia, and Canada, have embarked on the largest economic experiment of their history, which is the attempt to control their economies via their governments and

137

especially their central banks. They are trying to control their economies "from above" so to speak thinking that they have the power to direct the economy and influence the market forces as needed.

How will this experiment work? We will soon find out, but I venture to say it is already a bust. Why do I claim that? Well, look at the results: Massive debts throughout all the major economies. Reason? The "rough spots" or the ups and downs of the economy which they try to handle from above are not cushioned with new sophisticated systems or by newly trained "specialists" but by mere machination such as the printing of money and the government stepping in to boost their crony companies with tax dollars. This experiment is further pretended to work by the use of massive borrowing from all sources and as such we have massive debts in all areas of the economy, especially government debt.

Why all this nonsense? Because the politicians want to be the boss and Joe Public thinks all these good bureaucrats know best, have altruistic motives and will do the right things for them. Good luck to us all, may God help us.

The best way to cushion the natural ups and downs of the different sectors of an economy is to make it more of a true free enterprise system as explained in this book. The more free enterprise the economy is, the less it will be subjected to systemic ups and downs. In a true free enterprise system, although there will be natural recessions in some area of the economy, other sectors will be going up and as such it will constantly balance itself, while the totality of the economy continues to grow steadily. "Elementary, my dear Watson." More about that in the book *How to Fix Any Economy in the World.*

CAPITALISM AND THE WESTERN WORLD

The Western World claims to represent capitalism and to be proud of such. Well, the word *capitalism* was coined by Karl Marx and according to him it is a system whereby the rich people, the capitalists, make money at the detriment of the poor people. So, to use the word capitalism instead of free enterprise is like using the enemy's words to describe you. **When American's say: "We are proud of our capitalistic society", what they truly mean is that they proud of their free enterprise system.** As such, they should never use Karl Marx's word "capitalism" to describe it.

THE FUTURE OF AMERICAN DEBT

Government debt is sinister regardless of what uninformed people claim. "The government" is all of us as a country. How can anyone put "us" in debt without our consent? It's like parents putting their kids in debt without their knowledge.

Why should America, the richest country in the world, be in so much debt? I don't have a good answer or at least not a reasonable one but the debt does concern me greatly.

It is my humble opinion that the purpose of government debt is for control of you and me and nothing else. Yet some of my business friends tell me that since all of the American government debt is in U.S. dollars, it can be printed at any point by our treasury, and therefore we have nothing to worry about. Since this is theoretically true, many of the people in the U.S. do not worry much about the size of our government debt.

Well, two things on this issue:

1. In order to print the debt or inflate our way out of it, it would take phenomenal political will, and I don't see anyone willing to mastermind such plan.

2. If my theory about debt being used to control a country is correct, then here is the scenario I see: A few years from now, there will be a certain propaganda about how Americans are unfairly enjoying the fruits of the U.S. dollar being the international currency and how it is very unfair that they can print their way out of their true and lawful obligations, i.e. their debt. To "correct" such "injustice", the propaganda will proclaim, and in order to protect the poor lenders, the American government debt

should be pegged to some concoction of currencies or international units of currency. The type and name of it will not matter, but the result of such action will affect us greatly. The American government will not be allowed to print these international units of currencies, and therefore, from there on out the debt will become "solidified" and will hang over America and its future generations. As such, elections will no longer matter since the entire political and economic system will be designed around what is needed and wanted to "manage/pay off" this debt.

Do you think I am wrong about the above thought process? I certainly hope so, but we do have a precedent in Greece.

In 2010, Greece had a high debt, approximately the same percent to GDP as the U.S. does now. All that debt was private and could have been negotiated with its lenders, mostly European banks, and Greece and could have gotten out of the trap.

What actually happened to Greece is summarized in the following 3 steps:

1. A massive international propaganda campaign took place against Greece, the Greeks and their debt.
2. The then elected Greek government "gave up", whatever that meant, and instead of calling for new elections, a

non-elected interim government was "picked" to handle the crisis. **Emphasis on non-elected and picked.**

3. This "interim government" agreed to accept a "bailout" from the European governments. The "bailout" money was then used to pay off the European banks (get them off the hook so to speak) and the Greek debt was from there on out, owed to the governments of Europe, and it was no longer private debt. Therefore, the Europeans never bailed Greece out, but instead bailed out their own banks who leant money foolishly to socialist governments. With this agreement, this interim "government", settled Greece with an enormous debt without the ability to negotiate.

Soon after the "bailouts", the Greek debt in terms of GDP went up by 50%. Some kind of bailout, right? The structure of their non-negotiable debt imposed all sorts of regulations on the no longer free Greeks for many generations. Today, the Greeks are mostly working to pay taxes, which could amount to even as high as 80% for some people and/or businesses. **Also, the founders of democracy were forced to pay real estate taxes on their homes for the first time in their history.**

FUNNEL EVERYTHING THROUGH THE STATE

The state, the wannabe bosses, try to force every action by the people and especially economic activity to pass through them.

Do you want to start any kind of business endeavor? Well, the state needs to approve it one way or the other. Even menial jobs nowadays require licenses and degrees. How do you acquire the degrees? Well you must go to the universities which are controlled directly or indirectly by the state, where they "socially engineer" the students based on their own beliefs.

Thus, in order to be a mechanical engineer, for instance, you must also take courses in social sciences, which by itself is not a bad thing, but unlike engineering it is a very subjective subject. But, the "social scientists" at these universities don't think that social sciences are subjective and therefore you better not disagree with their viewpoints, otherwise they will give you an "F" on the subjective papers you have to write. **So, if you disagree with the "social engineers" points of view at the university you can't be a real engineer.**

Please reread the above paragraph as I cannot overemphasize it. This is insidious dystopia which gets very little, if any publicity. Wake up people, your freedoms are being taken away and you are not even aware, let alone fighting for them.

Chapter 12

THE FOUR PROBLEMS
SOCIALISM IS UNABLE TO OVERCOME

By now you probably determined that I do not like socialism and the whole idea of attempting to make people "equal." Actually, that would be incorrect. I do not dislike the idea of socialism nor am I against the idea of helping everyone and making our world a better and a fairer place to live in. In fact, I like a lot of things about socialism. For one, it takes care of poor relatives, gets all kids to school and promises security for all at least in the short run. Also, like a mesmerizing movie, it makes one forget the harshness of competition and the uncertainties of life on planet Earth.

On a personal note, my dad died when I was a teenager, and since I was the oldest of six children, I had to struggle to make a life for my family. It was very rough and very uncertain for a good long time. As such I would have liked for socialism to have taken care of me and my family.

Along the same line, if I was a god, I would make things easier for everyone. An easier life would perhaps not be to peoples' benefit in the long run, but I don't like to see people suffer either. In terms of helping people, I find myself to be more of a socialist than the proclaimed ones. I am involved with all sorts of causes and organizations, local, national, and international which help people of all kinds in all aspects of life. Anti-drug campaigns, improving education, improving governments, etc., etc.

Then, why is it that I do not advocate socialism as a political system and as the best means to govern people? It is because it is not truthful and as such it does not work and will never work. **In fact, socialism in any form causes harm for anyone who engages in it. It is so insidious whereby people don't even know the harm it causes until it is too late.**

Why is socialism so unworkable? It is because it cannot overcome the following four problems in regard to its implementation.

1. **You can't take people's money, or creative potential, without their agreement.**

   As a general rule, in a free enterprise democratic system, the people who earn more, provide a higher level of exchange with society than the ones who earn less. So, in order to give people equal benefits, you need to take from the ones who earn more and give it to the ones who earn less. The people who earn more are usually smarter than the bureaucrats who try to take it away from them and they will not allow for this to happen. If you look at history, you will see that when people find out that they will get taxed more than 30% of their overall possible earnings, or better said, their potential output or creation, they will do one or some of the following four things:

a. Show less income, legally or illegally.

b. Leave the country or move their company out of the country

c. Use their talents to get benefits other than monetary gain which cannot be taxed. In the middle ages able men joined the priesthood to protect themselves from governments.

d. Put on a "sombrero" and go to sleep, or a swimsuit and go to the beach, instead of working hard day and night, to the detriment of all.

Many socialistic governments around the world are **claiming** to be taxing their high earners more than 50%. Well, look closer at these places who claim such and you will see that any of the above four things is occurring despite the fact that the government is claiming otherwise. As mentioned earlier in the book, a few years back, I saw an article in a magazine, possibly *The Economist*, that in "socialistic" Sweden, ABBA, the popular music group paid the most taxes than any single organization or company for that year. What about all these other multibillion-dollar companies Sweden has? How could they show less income than Abba? My point exactly. They applied one or all of the four dodges against money confiscation. How do the smart Greeks avoid paying the extremely high taxes levied by their government today? They just leave the country, that's how.

2. Socialism cannot incentivize people to cause growth in the economy.

Any economy is made up of INCENTIVES. People must have incentives to cause growth and expansion of any kind. NO INCENTIVES, No Growth, No Research, no expansion ... nothingness.

Some people believe in the idea of, "He who has two of something is to give the extra to a fellow who has none." That sounds good as a superficial and cursory look but if analyzed in depth this brings about socialism and death to any economy. The reason being that, if the law or moral code of the land is that you give your extra of anything to another, then once you got your own one of something, will you continue to create that extra since you are expected to give it to someone else? For example, say you have a house and want an additional one as an investment to rent out or just wanted an additional house for yourself, will you work and build that other one just to give it to another? I doubt it. Once you get your one "house" or one of anything, you will find excuses not to create another one regardless of how able you are to the detriment of all.

3. **In Socialism, the government becomes the custodian and manager of the money in the economy.**

    The taxes the government gets is paid by the most successful companies of the land. This money belongs to the employers and employees of these companies. **These are the most successful producers and money managers in the country.** Socialism assumes that the government bureaucrats will put these monies to better use for the benefit of the country than its true owners. That is just silly! It's not based on logic.

4. **Socialistic countries cannot force other countries to follow socialism and stand still.**

    While Greece was basking in socialistic glory in the 1980's and 1990's other countries around them were growing by leaps and bounds. They were doing research and creating great companies while Greece was becoming more and more dependent on other countries' products. Results? Non-competitive companies and a non-competitive work force which caused a collapse of the Greek economy relative to its competitors.

    You see, the world is made up of competition based on games and the pursuit of survival and glory. It's not based on "let's all be friends." You can't stop competition just because you or your country thought something "humane" to implement. For example, socialistic Greece enforces a siesta rule whereby most commercial businesses must close between 2-5 p.m. Why? Because they claim it contributes to a more humane existence. That's fine but that rule causes a lot of lost productivity especially for the young people who want to create a life for themselves. Most importantly though, can the socialistic Greek government enforce its competitors in other countries to have a siesta and halt that much productivity as well, so that Greece does not fall behind? Of course it cannot. By the way, can Greece even force all of its own people to take a siesta? No, it cannot, and there lies another big lie of socialism, which is that even some of the enforcers do not take "siestas" while they tell you to do so. Instead they try to get ahead while pretending to be standing still.

The way socialists try to fix these four problems is by globalization. They want to force everyone to be socialists otherwise their socialistic experiment will not work, and they will look foolish, see Cuba. Therefore, they force the entire world to be socialistic, no sorry, I meant globalized, No, no, sorry again, I meant coercing us to be "One Big Happy Family", yes that's it. Now I got it! **Globalization is forced on the world by socialists, regardless if we want to be part**

of it or not, in order to solve the above four problems and especially problem #4 and for no other reason.

The reason I am not a socialist is because socialism does not work. What works is a True Free Enterprise system in a responsible democracy as this is truthful and most closely resembles the true nature of the world which is made up of unevenness, ambitions, games, incentives, problems, barriers and rewards. **Truth is workable and therefore it creates the best possible outcome. Socialism is a nontruth and thus it creates long-term misery, failure and ultimate slavery no matter the pretenses.**

CHAPTER 13
THE BASIC REASONS TOTALITARIAN
SYSTEMS DO NOT WORK

The real reasons totalitarian systems don't work are:

1. WE ARE NOT CREATED EQUAL. No one person is equal to any other person in terms of abilities, desires, wants, ambitions, vision, etc.
2. We are motivated by self-interest toward self-preservation and survival for now and for the future.
3. We are spiritual beings who want to expand individually and as a group. Expansion is what makes people happy, not stagnation and mediocrity.

As such, anyone who is half alive in this world, wants to create things, own these creations, and enjoy the fruits of his labor.

Given the above facts, how do you devise a governing system that works? Any way you look at it, only a free enterprise system as described in this book can work.

If a totalitarian system forces a smart and ambitious guy or girl to work hard and give his blood, sweat and tears to another person, who does not work as hard, without a fair exchange, will try to cheat the system or will not create as much as he could. The very people who say that they can force another to create without incentives, are the ones who will not do it either. Take this to the bank! It has never happened, and it will never happen in the history of mankind. Period!

But in a true free enterprise system, a fellow who owns his own creation like his own company and feels that he will be rewarded greatly and unevenly for his great and uneven efforts; will go out of his way to help less fortunate people, in this case his employees, because they will contribute to his own ambitions and survival. A win-win system. "Elementary, my Dear Watson."

I can write an entire book on this, but if you confront what is written above you can spare the reading of a couple hundred pages.

Here I want to clarify a couple of points. When I say we are not created equal, please understand that I also believe the following:

a. The judicial system needs to treat people equally regardless of circumstances, especially when it comes to criminal law.

b. We are equal in the eyes of God. We better be, He made us. Anything else would be like a parent treating his kids with prejudice and that's not God-like. Along this line and joking aside, one spiritual being is not less than another spiritual being and as such no one is better or greater than another. We are sacred, spiritual entities without body color or even ethnicity. As such, we are responsible for each other and our physical world, i.e. Earth, as we progress into the future. All we are addressing here, is

155

how to devise a governing system that best manages what is found in the nature of man, which is, uneven abilities and ambitions.

Look at the following graphs which fully explain the above concepts.

The State of Mankind

The numbers are arbitrary. Some talents are known, others are unknown.

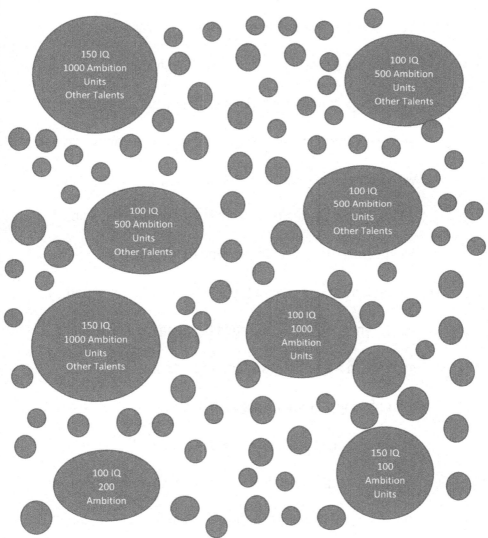

If this is what is found in nature, then you only have three options to arrange or govern "the group" you see in the graph.

a. You allow them to be, without rules or official governance, which means they will end up literally fighting it out, where the "strongest man" wins. That is an uncontrolled revolution and every man for himself type of thing. At the end everyone will bow to the strongest leader, until someone stabs him, and a new guy takes over. That is the rule of the jungle. Most people will object to this type of system; or

b. A hierarchy of sorts. Here I repeat the totalitarian hierarchy as shown in the previous pages because it's what usually happens in a hierarchy system, regardless of its name. A lot of people promote this system by saying that the most able or the most productive ones should run things for the world to be right. Well, that's good in theory but who decides that Joe is more able than Bill and based on what criteria? Usually is because Joe is more forceful, bold and audacious and nothing more. But even if we get it right in terms of ability and leadership today, will that hold true a year from now when things in the marketplace or the overall environment have changed? Also, there is no guarantee of good succession either. So, this hierarchy business is very risky. In addition, people are not happy to be labeled as anything and are not happy when they think they are just peons or mere mortals as in the ancient Greek world of the gods and mortals.

A TOTALITARIAN HIERARCHY AND

WHAT ACTUALLY HAPPENS IN SUCH A SYSTEM

A COMMUNIST OR A FASCIST COUNTRY

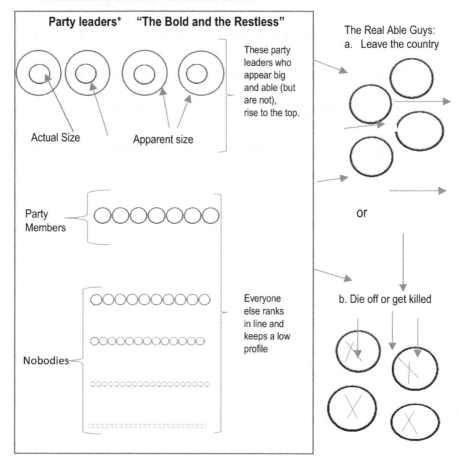

Party leaders*   **"The Bold and the Restless"**

These party leaders who appear big and able (but are not), rise to the top.

Actual Size   Apparent size

The Real Able Guys:
a. Leave the country

Party Members

Everyone else ranks in line and keeps a low profile

Nobodies

or

b. Die off or get killed

*Party leaders

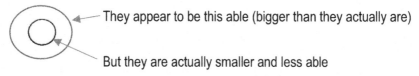

They appear to be this able (bigger than they actually are)

But they are actually smaller and less able

This leaves us with the third option.

c. A free enterprise system, where people are allowed to arrange themselves in teams, competing and exchanging with each other in a responsible democracy, as explained in the book, "**What is Wrong with Democracy and How to Fix It.**"

This free enterprise system:

1. Produces the best possible governance for people.

2. Constantly offers the best form of leadership the market requires at any given time.

3. People are the happiest as they always have a chance to move about and change their job situation or life as they wish, and nothing is set in stone.

4. No one can label anyone, including myself as in this book, as being lesser or greater than anyone else. Since we all have different abilities and different talents, as the market changes, so do the chances for each person's talents and abilities to shine.

A TRUE FREE ENTERPRISE SYSTEM

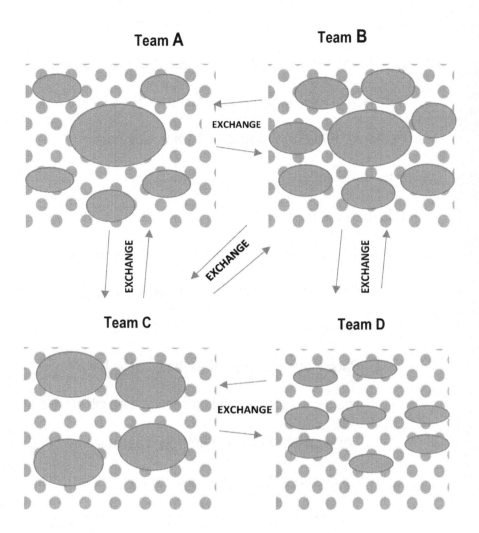

Different teams, with people of vastly different abilities with various configurations and matches. The arrows represent exchange of ideas products and services. **The team members have vast choices among teams since a true free-enterprise system has no monopolies or oligopolies in it.**

CHAPTER 14

THE TWO MAIN MOTIVATORS
AND MOVERS IN LIFE

Life is a game, as such there is movement and it involves energy. There is a thrust toward a future. What are the elements of that thrust and what does this game involve? It involves self-preservation and promulgation. It involves the playing of the game in teams and individually, but mostly in teams. The team which is suited best for the occasion wins. The team gets the "trophy" since they toppled the enemy and they are now on top and feel safe in that they will survive into the future.

But, what are life's most popular games? What causes the most movement of energy and resources? Otherwise said, what causes the most excitement?

By observation the two main motivators and movers in life are **enterprising ventures, i.e. business, and war**, interlaced with sex and religion. The Trojan War, written by Homer in the Iliad, the oldest known western literature piece, had all the above elements in it. The Greeks went to fight the Trojans who charged too much for passage to the Black Sea, so it involved business and war. Helen added romance and the gods (religion) were also in play.

You can get people to do stuff in the name of religion, help, sex, forced labor, etc.; but what really motivates people and gets them to go beyond and above and to push their limits, is either business, as in the pursuit of gain for self and group, or war for group gain or protection. **Therefore, in order to motivate people,**

you need to use business or war with the emotions of greed or fear which can exist in both.

The best of times is when business dominates as the game. The worst of times is when war is the predominate game. **These two elements, business enterprises and war, move humanity the most.** They move man to extremes and cause him to do the unthinkable. They can dominate all the resources and energy in the land. Yes, religion and sex can also move humanity but these are not the primary movers.

If the above is true, then the only thing that makes sense to me is to use business, in a free enterprise and democratic system, as the main motivator and route for the long-term progress and survival of mankind.

The hierarchy of forced collectivism and fascism are not positive primary movers for people, because they suppress personal gain and the pleasure that comes with it. What humans want is a game in which they can expand and get gain for themselves and their group. Collectivism and fascism no matter the size of their drums and propaganda, do not inspire great motivation because they are not about personal gain and the freedom that comes with it. **Since totalitarian systems are not about free enterprise creations, they ultimately use the other motivator, war, and as such they cause people to die a miserable death either in actual war, stagnation or starvation.**

CHAPTER 15

WHAT DOES CIVILIZATION, FREEDOM, AND JUSTICE DEPEND ON?

Our goals with free enterprise and democracy are a civilization*
where freedom and justice are the pillars of society. So, how does
this come about?

**Civilization, freedom and justice is based on the
following four elements:**

1. **A democratic true free enterprise system.**
2. **True Education about life. (See Freedom Intelligences,** in
   Intelligence: Discover the 65 Traits of Intelligence)
3. **Balance of power.** No single entity, be it private or
   governmental, should control directly or indirectly more than
   20% of any sector of the economy in any part of the country (see
   pertinent chapter).
4. **No deficits or debts**
   a. No trade deficits with other countries and
   b. No budget deficits which lead to government debt and
      consequent enslavement of its people.

If you don't have the above four elements in place you can't
have a civilized society but will have either a mob of thieves or a
bunch of scared people following a suppressive overpowering
regime. Also, you will not have win-win exchanges but mostly win-
lose deals as when the government prints money and hands it out to
specific groups such as Bankers.

A few years back I commissioned a Greek Scholar to do a research on how Democracy came about in ancient Athens. He wrote an entire historical thesis for me about Solon, Clisthenes, Pericles and all the old boys in Ancient Athenian Era who put the whole thing together. Well it was all good historical data, but **what I got out of it** was that although these were great thinkers and great leaders, **no one single person developed Democracy, but rather there was a critical mass of enlightened people who were "standing tall" and Democracy came about as the natural political system these people agreed to be governed with. What does that remind you of? An enlightened critical mass of people at the beginnings of America. The American forefathers.**

During both times democracy came about naturally as it made the most sense to these enlightened people as it being the most logical political system to be governed by.

Thus, when you have enlightened people in any area, democracy, justice and true free enterprise are the natural consequences of the mix. But if we create a mob of suppressed individuals, then the place becomes Barbarism and as a consequence they will seek more government to survive better, or so they think.

Therefore, if we want democracy, free enterprise and justice we need a critical mass of enlightened people and thus **the purpose of this book.**

169

What are the characteristics of enlightened people?

1. Citizens who are educated about responsible democracy and true free enterprise.
2. Freedom loving individuals who believe and defend free enterprise and democracy
3. Capable
4. Self-reliant
5. Responsible citizens
6. People with a strong culture and belief system
7. Ones who believe in the spirituality of man and in a higher power and do not see themselves as lone wolfs or wild animals in the wilderness.
8. They seek win-win exchanges (civilized* people).

*Definition of Civilization: How do we define civilization or civilized people? Is it about having good roads? Great looking buildings? Or shiny cars? When people think of civilization, they also think in terms of being civil, or polite and kind to others. They further assume that with the passage of time due to our experiences "deposited in our DNA", we get more and more civilized. That is not true, humans have not evolved from apes and human nature has not changed in thousands of years despite the technological advancements.

Civilized I call the people who exhibit the following four characteristics:

1. **They attempt win-win exchanges and as such**
2. **Believe in fairness in all of their dealings**
3. **They do what they have agreed to do, and**
4. **To obtain the above, they seek the truth in agreements and about life in general.**

If a society does not exhibit the above characteristics or exhibits the opposite, I call them barbarians.

If the above is needed for the existence of the free enterprise system, we also need to know how it is lost by looking at what conditions must exist for socialism, communism, or fascism to come about.

Chapter 16

WHAT IS NEEDED FOR TOTALITARIAN SYSTEMS TO COME INTO EXISTENCE?

The growth of socialism, communism or fascism depends on the following:

1. The creation of an underclass* which needs big brother, i.e. a large government or big corporations to support it.

   *Underclass: a) maimed individuals, i.e. broken families, people involved in criminal activity, etc. b) poorly educated about a job and most importantly, not educated about life. c) They have no strong culture and they can easily be lied to and swayed by the mass media or other organizations. d) Since poorly educated they cannot produce and therefore are unable to survive without the help of big government.

2. The creation of an uprooted society which has no cultural identity or strong beliefs about themselves or their group.

3. Lots of immoral groups of people, who seek win-lose exchanges.

4. The bombarding of society with false information about anything to do with people, life, and spirituality with the goal of control.

5. A polarized society; the creation of us and them. The "Haves" and "Have nots." One Race against another. "The protected ones" and the "unprotected others." The unprotected desire protection and big brother is there ready to provide it.

False information and polarization are key elements for a totalitarian system to come about. They push people toward a predetermined goal, such as revolution.

Looking at history, the totalitarian systems which were created by people like Hitler, Stalin, and Mao had all of the above elements in place. These barbarians did not act alone, they or others had created thousands of henchmen who agreed with their suppressive plans.

But you say: How could this be? Socialism is supposed to be by the people for all the people with a long-term plan to create a Utopia on planet earth, is it not? Well, this is the main lie as they claim that their totalitarian system is supposed to make things equal for all and that the "Socialistic Democracy", "The Socialist Republic" or "The People's Liberation Army", whatever the euphemistic name used by the communistic or fascists, was created by the people.

Despite all the attempts to convince people otherwise, the truth is that **Communism and fascism, the best-known totalitarian systems, do not come about from the people at large, but rather from suppressive elitists with a plan to control others and who claim and pretend to do it all in the name of helping them. These elitists know full well that communism and fascism destroy the psyche of the people create barbarians, but**

that is exactly what they want since they are about control and nothing else. Please don't take my word for it, look at history.

THE FUNNIEST THING ABOUT REVOLUTIONARIES

The most laughable thing about the excited (fanatic) totalitarian supporters, i.e. fascists, socialists, communists, or religious warriors, is the absence of the following lack of computation which is: When the revolutionary dust settles there has to be some kind of a system to organize society anew. Such as, having people in charge governing the rest of us. But without democracy and free enterprise these revolutionaries in charge of XYZ totalitarian system, will have to be omniscient about life and people in it. We know that is not possible. Therefore, the result of their revolution, which had as its goal to obtain freedom from, brings slavery at the end.

Anything which destroys true free enterprise and democracy brings about totalitarian systems which always create slavery.

Not to be redundant, but the only workable political and governing system is true free enterprise in a responsible democracy*. In such a system no omniscience is needed. It is self-balancing and self-correcting. Amen!

*See the book *What's Wrong with Democracy and How to Fix It.*

PLOTS, PLANS, CONSPIRACIES AND HIDDEN DATA

If you talk about conspiracies or planned out plots, you will be immediately ridiculed by the socialists and will be considered paranoid. But why is that? Because they don't want you to look for secret plots and discover their plans.

This is an old trick and it goes back to the story of Iliad. The book was written by Homer and it is the first known literature of the western world. It was written, according to Aristotle, around 3,000 BC, much earlier than the 700 BC the historians proclaim.

Iliad is the story of the Trojan War. The Greeks against the Persians, Achilles vs Hector, Menelaos vs Paris, etc. Hundreds of pages cover this story and most people know about it via readings or movies. But what most do not know about, is that the war between the Greeks and Persians is only half the text. The other half covers what the gods were doing during that war or contest. They were plotting and conspiring to help either the Greeks or the Persians, and had their own games, which affected both sides. These were the unseen players in this game called the Trojan War. So, why would people not know about this part of the book? Because it is unbelievable and unexplainable with our awareness of today. So, we leave it alone. We don't talk about it. We don't present it. We don't teach it. But it is in plain sight, it is in the book, Homer wrote it for us.

Well, it is the same thing with other plots and conspiracies of today. We don't want to accept such. We are also told that they are not true. Really? Why not? Life is a game. In playing games, we have plans, plots, conspiracies and hidden data. So, if you want to be a free and aware person, you need to look up and accept what you observe and not what they force you to accept as truth.

Do you know why the "important" people in our society don't believe in conspiracies? It is because they feel important and believe that if there was anything of the nature of conspiracy, they, would know all about it. Really? You mean an "important" professor at a university making $150,000 per year would know all about things because he is a professor? And you mean a guy who earns $1 billion per year and has friends of the same wealth would consider the professor important enough to tell him all about his plots and conspiracies? That's laughable.

There are people among us with tremendous power, secret knowledge and hidden plots. They have their plans, which may not align with our plans for individual freedom. So, what is our defense? I suggest free enterprise and democracy. They can combat any conspiracies and can help maintain our liberties. You decide.

In Ronald Regan's words:
"Freedom is never more than one generation from extinction."

Chapter 17

How to Handle People who Think, Talk, and Act Irrationally

In the previous chapter we talked about how totalitarianism comes about and discovered that at its core is misinformation. When given false information, people's thought processes become jumbled up and they end up thinking, talking, and acting irrationally. Logical and properly informed people, get stunned with this kind of irrational behavior and don't understand how others could behave this way and are not sure how to combat such irrationality.

The main reason people are irrational about an issue is because they are missing data or have been given false data about the subject of discussion. Real data defined as: True facts about a subject.

The wrong thing to do with these people is to attack their belief system. **Why? Because they have formulated their position or viewpoint about the subject based on erroneous data or at least not the data that you have. So first and foremost, you must discover the information they are computing with, about the subject in discussion, and who gave it to them, instead of combating their beliefs or conclusions about it.**

When debating geopolitical issues for example, you don't disagree with their beliefs about these issues, but you ask questions. Such as: "Do you know what the GDP* of the US is? How about the Chinese or Canadian GDP? Who are our biggest training partners? (currently it's China and Canada) What bracket of the population pays most of the federal taxes in the USA? In your opinion what made America special compared to other countries? You can further ask if they know which country has the most natural resources and ask if they know what that country's GDP is. If that country's GDP is low, inquire if they know as to what contributed to such a small economy despite all the resources. In addition to the above, ask for undisputed historical data which you know well. You can also ask them questions about politics and economics from data you got in this book.

If during the discussion someone disagrees with you on fair trade and instead supports free trade, you ask if he knows what the trade deficit of our country is with the country in question and what the long-term ramifications will be for us because of this deficit. Most Americans have no idea that the U.S. in 2018 had a trade deficit of over $350 billion dollars with China. That number is rising every year. Three hundred and fifty billion is more than the entire GDP of most countries. This will not end well for the U.S, and someone will get hurt because of this imbalance in trade with China

*GDP =   1. Gross Domestic Product

2. The cost of goods and services exchanging hands throughout the country per year

3. The yearly economic output of a country.

Essentially, you are trying to figure out what data they have about things and the world at large which caused them to formulate their opinion on the geopolitical issues you are discussing with them. Also find out who gave these data to them.

In another example, when you are dealing with a person who is promoting the benefits of socialism, instead of rebutting their position on the subject, just ask him or her about basic data in regard to socialism. Ask and find out; what their definition of socialism is. Or what is one to expect from a socialistic government or the economy under such a system? You will be shocked from their answers.

Unfortunately, most people don't read books, nor can they observe properly, so they accept mass media propaganda conclusions instead of getting true data via truthful sources or clear observations in life. This propaganda they are "inhaling" gives them emotional ideas about stuff but without true data, observable in life.

So, if you run into a person who is irrational about geopolitical issues or any issues for that matter, don't debate him/her on their beliefs or ideas about the subject, but calmly question their data or true knowledge about it instead. You will always find, that they have missing or wrong data about the subject.

It would go like this: You ask about their data on the subject, then ask for more data and also find out who gave these to them; and pull the string to discover their ignorance or erroneous information about it. After that you can painstakingly attempt to educate them and correct the false information they have. **By correcting one's false data about a subject and replacing it with the correct data, you will cave in one's entire wrong computation or philosophical belief about it.**

The above process might take a few discussions but there is no other way to correct someone's incorrect philosophical beliefs on a subject. This book should be able to do all this work for you.

A graphic depiction of the above is presented on the following page.

But if you find that the person is unwilling to look at the possibility of other data, then realize that you are dealing with a barbarian and you need to deal with him accordingly. See pertinent chapter ahead.

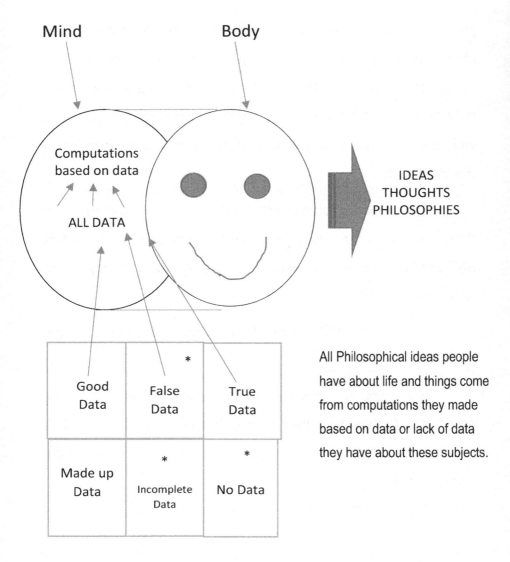

Mind   Body

Computations
based on data

ALL DATA

IDEAS
THOUGHTS
PHILOSOPHIES

Good Data	False Data	True Data
Made up Data	Incomplete Data	No Data

All Philosophical ideas people have about life and things come from computations they made based on data or lack of data they have about these subjects.

Data one has received on different subjects

Each box represents a different subject.

*In order to correct the false ideas on has about a subject, you must first correct the false or incorrect information they have about it and then replace it with the correct data.

HOW IS IT THAT PEOPLE ARE GIVEN FALSE DATA?

As mentioned in the book *Intelligence: Discover the 65 Traits of Intelligence*, the school systems as they are set up around the world today for the most part are not educating* people on the freedom intelligences. **As such the world at large is ignorant about politics, economics and the importance of democracy and free enterprise. Thus, the purpose of these books.**

It has been said that people don't get the government they need but the government they deserve based on their knowledge and responsibility level. So, my purpose and mission is to educate people and increase their knowledge about free enterprise and democracy and cause people to increase their responsibility level so that they can create a government that will bring about a Golden Age and not a totalitarian regime.

*Besides the freedom intelligences, most schools do not even educate students on being able to read or write properly. Please realize that, although the words in this book are not very difficult, if you truly understand what you are reading here, you belong to the top 5% of society. Hard to believe, but a sad truth.

Chapter 18

FREEDOM vs SLAVERY

Life is a game and if you win, the prize is freedom but, if you lose, the punishment is slavery. But what are the tools to win freedom and how does one protect himself from becoming a slave? I cover this in chapter L "Freedom and Intelligence" in the book *"Intelligence: Discover the 65 traits of Intelligence"*. There I present the seven pillars of freedom and the seven elements of slavery. Since this book is about freedom versus to totalitarianism I am repeating these here as well, in the following pages.

1. WHAT DOES FREEDOM DEPEND ON?

Freedom Depends on the Following Seven Pillars:

1. **The understanding that competition in life is constant**
2. **The realization that we need Democracy and Free Enterprise.**
3. **Responsibility**
4. **Knowledge**
5. **Ability**
6. **Team Support**
7. **Production**

This holds true for an individual as well as for a nation. Explained further,

1. **Life is a game.** *For any game to have interest, there must be competition.* **As such, one must realize that competition in the game of life is constant.** *If you think otherwise, it's like*

*hoping that the other team will go to sleep. If it does, then you hope that the next team will also go to sleep, same for the other one, and so on and so forth. As you see, the logistics are against you. So if you want to be free, accept the fact that competition is and will always be constant. **So, never put your guard down.***

*2. Further, you must realize that everyone you meet has different viewpoints and different realities. If you think that someone in charge of a totalitarian regime will be an angel or a saint and that he will have the best at heart for you and your family, you are very much mistaken. The smooth-talking politician is not as smart, able, or as hard working as you might think. **Therefore, to be free, you need democracy in order to have a say so in your governance and a free enterprise system to have the freedom to create energy which at this point in our society is money. This comes about by low taxation, limited government, limited and sensical regulations. Also, you need a philosophy that promotes wealth creation and not misery.***

*3. **You need to take responsibility for your right to be free;** NO ONE else will do it for you. If you give up that responsibility others will gladly use your slave labor.*

*4. Therefore, you need to obtain the necessary **knowledge** that is needed to survive optimally in the environment you find yourself in and*

*5. **gain the necessary abilities** required to create and maintain your freedom. Without the ability to create exchangeable products and services, with others you will not be able to maintain your freedom, but you will soon be enslaved.*

*6. No matter how able you might be, **you need a proper team, because life is a game, and games are played by teams**. The best team wins. Said otherwise **you need allies**. Allies are not necessarily friends. Friends are not necessarily allies; they might just be friends. Your team is your family, co-workers, partners, and the rest of your countrymen. You must accept the responsibility to create your team. Always!*

*7. But you can't just sit there and look pretty in your team's uniform. **You and your team need to create products and services to exchange with the world. Exchange is your ticket to life's game**. Without it you can't get in the arena. Thus, you need to produce goods and services in abundance as needed so you don't depend on others for survival.*

190

If you check the above in life and throughout history, you will see that they hold true. If it is so, then the opposite would be the road to slavery.

2. WHAT DOES SLAVERY DEPEND ON?

When people talk of slavery in America, they think of racial slavery and something of the past. That's inaccurate. All peoples and races throughout the world have been enslaved, to a lesser or greater degree. The Greeks and Romans called the Northern Europeans barbarians and treated them badly. In turn, Greeks were enslaved by the Romans and the Ottomans.

Enslavement is the overwhelm and the inability to do something about it. Enslavement takes many different forms, some are less obvious than others. Peoples throughout history were enslaved because they were unable to protect themselves from others, who overwhelmed them.

The purpose of this writing is to lay out the anatomy of slavery and how to protect oneself from being overwhelmed by others. The seven necessary elements for slavery to take place are:

1. *Thinking that all competition is extinct or that it will be extinct soon.*

2. *The absence of democracy and free enterprise*

3. *Lack of responsibility*

4. *Lack of knowledge*

5. *Disabled people*

6. *No team or a bad team*

7. *Lack of production*

1. *As mentioned in the previous pages, the logistics that all competition will stop in the universe are impossible.* Competition is constant. So, if anyone is telling you otherwise, he is trying to put you and your team to sleep for the benefit of the competitor.

2. There are many good people in the world who do great things for our society, but **to think that a leader of a totalitarian regime will be an angel or a saint and that he will lead you to the promised land is a terrible miscalculation.** Absolute power corrupts, always. To be free you need options. **You need democracy and free enterprise always!**

In order to create a slave society they must suppress the people's ability to have energy/money in any form. This comes in the form of high taxation, unlimited government, *nonsensical laws and regulations, pretended democracy and lack of free enterprise. **Also, the preaching that money is bad, or that wealth creation is unnecessary.***

*3. If you **don't take the responsibility** to educate yourself about life and freedom in general, you will*

*4. **lack the knowledge** needed to be free and you will be **unable** to function successfully.*

*5. **The most important ingredient for slavery is weak, unable or disabled people**[1]. Able[2] people will always fight enslavement; disabled ones will gladly put on the handcuffs and accept any type of enslavement just to get a meal for themselves or their families.*

*6. If you act as a lone wolf and **without a team backing you up, you will be easily overwhelmed**. Lack of team support makes you vulnerable to the slave masters whose objective is to divide and conquer so that they can overwhelm you. Bad schooling, bad diet, misinformation, splintering people from their teams, such as in divorce and therefore broken teams (families) create **weak and vulnerable people** who will be glad to serve masters in the hopes of obtaining survival.*

---

[1] Weak or disabled people: The people who lack some or most of the seven pillars of freedom.
[2] Able People: The ones who possess the seven pillars of freedom.

193

Our society today has not been indoctrinated in the concept of the need to create a team and as such people are trying to survive without one. Observe how little they are involved in civic affairs.

*7. If one is **not in a position to produce** any valuable products or services to exchange with society he will be dependent on others for his survival.*

The words slavery and slave master have very bad connotations in our society. Therefore, any slavery creation units cannot advertise as such, but they must go under different names. Can you think of people or institutions who are instrumental in doing 1—7 above? Well, whatever name they go under, realize that they are slave creation units.

If you got the idea that socialism and globalization require and therefore promote, all of the above elements, then you get to go to the front of the class.

The biggest lie of Communism or Socialism is that it's something which is created by the people. That's a total lie. Socialism and Communism are formulas which are rolled out and used when desired. The purpose of communism or socialism, as it's called today, a more palatable word, is created by power hungry elitists who want to:

194

a. Control the people

   And/or

b. "Freeze" areas for a long time and put them out of competition. See what they did to Ancient Athens, Russia, Cuba or Venezuela.

Chapter 19

HOW DOES BARBARISM COME ABOUT?

HOW DOES BARBARISM COME ABOUT?

A barbarian is someone who:

   a. Is not looking for mutual gain, but rather for a win for him and a loss for others.
   b. He will not do what he promised and agreed to do for or with others.
   c. Therefore, he does not care about fairness and justice and
   d. Consequently, he does not care about the truth in things or life.

As such, barbarians think that life is a zero-sum game and try to win over other peoples' losses. Since, they do not do what they have agreed to do, they do not care about fairness and justice. Consequently, they do not care about the truth either.

Because a lot of people around the world talk about win-win deals and praise freedom and democracy, it would appear that this is the accepted norm and it is what the majority of people advocate. Alas, the world is mostly ruled by barbarians and not free enterprise democratic thinkers.

How does barbarism come about? It is a simple mathematical equation. It goes like this: I want to take what you have, or I want you to do XYZ for me, because I feel it would benefit me in some way. So, I push to get my way. If I get little or no resistance, I keep taking without proper exchange with you or anyone else until something or someone stops me. That's barbarism.

If I get resistance and I can't get what I want without an exchange, then I will be forced to provide an exchange and make it a win-win deal with others so that I can eventually get what I want or need. That's called civilization.

Free enterprise systems and democracy create constant competition, and plenty of choices. In such a system, everyone is compelled to create win-win deals in order to survive well, and in the process, create a civilized culture as defined in this book.

Totalitarian systems, big government, socialism, monopolies and oligopolies, create win-lose deals, a barbarian culture, since no one can push back against a behemoth government or a huge business monopoly. As such, they also "indoctrinate" people to create win-lose deals among each other. This is called barbarism by contamination.

It is really that simple, and although the good people in our society think that the majority want win-win deals and free enterprise, they are mistaken as this is not the norm. Sadly, the majority of people are not looking for win-win deals and have no clue of the importance of free enterprise and democracy. Either because they are already winning at other people's expense or because they are ignorant about the basics of life, and more specifically about individual freedom and democracy.

Therefore, the people who fully appreciate free enterprise and responsible democracy, need to defend and protect their freedoms, as others will not do it for them, due to the above reasons. The freedom advocates will have to educate others about the benefits of a democratic society which advances free enterprise.

The good news is that, although a lot of people can act like barbarians in a barbaric society, most will revert to acting civilized as soon as they can, if a system is no longer oppressive.

So, once the system is fixed, i.e. democracy and free enterprise become the norm, the clouds depart and the sun of civilization shines through. See golden ages around the world during the last 5000 years of history.

But, a small percentage, like 5% of the people, despite our best efforts to educate or indoctrinate them to a win-win system, they will continue to act like barbarians, regardless of circumstances or how well they are treated. Instead, they will continuously attempt to take down and destroy others just because they feel it suits them. **I call these people the Chronic Barbarians.** Why do these people continue to act like barbarians no matter the circumstance? Well, that's a whole other study, but the above is a fact for anyone with the willingness to confront such.

So how do we deal with the chronic barbarians?

First of all, let me say that the above data is not known to most people and it is also not believable by most. People in general are trained to believe/think that all members of a society mean well as long as they are treated fairly. They are also taught that there are always two sides of any story. Another fixed idea people hold as truth is that, when there is smoke there is always fire.

Well, I am here to tell you that not everyone means well. Sometimes there is only one side to a story and the other side is just a lie or an insane computation. Hitler and Stalin were not reasonable people and never intended to be. Their story did not have a correct side. It was simply murder and mayhem. Further, just because there is smoke it does not necessarily mean that there is a fire there; sometimes it is just smoke.

So, when the chronic barbarians "come to the gate" and are after your freedom, your money, your house or country, there is nothing to reason with. For example, if I was to go on TV to debate a communist or a fascist, although I would present my views to the public, I would never debate such a person. To debate a liar and an unreasonable individual who is after my freedom is like arguing with a mad dog. That is crazy, you don't do that. What do you do instead? Well, the ancient Greeks had a saying: "When logos, which means logical discussion or logical arguments, is not acceptable, then you use a stick."

That is how you deal with the chronic barbarians, you use a stick and you make sure you protect yourself and your friends from them. Do it fast and do it swiftly as you can't reason with them because:

    a. They are not interested in being civil or fair
    b. They are just too lazy to be anything but barbarisms
    c. They are too crazy, regardless how sane they look
    d. All of the above.

How do you know who they are? You look at their actions and the results of these actions. They are the ones who tell you there is no right or wrong, and that the constitution does not matter. They are the people who feel democracy is to be used by them and not something to be respected as a fair system.

Don't fall prey to the idea that everyone has a right to do as they please. When people attack your freedoms and your sane environment you have every right and obligation to protect yourself and your friends.

So, don't be a victim. Use a stick when logic is no longer accepted, and the barbarians are at your "gate". Unless of course you want to commit suicide, which some people think is a noble thing to do; I happen not to be one of them.

This is the entire premise of the 2nd Amendment. It says the right to bear arms, but arms are not necessarily guns. In today's society, guns can be very useless and can be used against you. Arms means protection. The best protection/arm/stick at this time is the use of the legal system and legal means.

One of my friends told me that his daughter got an "F" on a subjective paper at school because she used the word "God" in her paper. The "F" was upheld by the Dean. A staff member was upset recently because her son said to her that a lot of his teachers have stated in the classroom that communism is the best form of government.

In both of these instances the school and teachers are out of line. They are there to teach the students what they signed up for, not their political philosophies. A public school is not there to socially engineer society based on some elitists thought processes. Another argument for a private education system.

Guns will not fix these issues. **It's the legal system we need to use heavily to stop and abolish this nonsense and restore freedom of speech and true democracy. Also, we need to get politically involved at all levels. More about that in the next chapter.**

Chapter 20
Your Responsibility

If what you have read thus far makes any sense to you then, in my humble or not so humble opinion, you are one of the few true sane people running around on this planet today. That is the good news. The bad news is that most people do not see what you see. If you wish to live in a free enterprise democracy, then you need to roll up your sleeves and fight for such a system; since the other people will not do it for you. They will not put out the needed effort, either because they do not see what you see or because they are not brave enough to confront slavery or that they feel they cannot make a difference. For an explanation on this, I am enclosing the chapter, "The Political Will of the People" taken from the book, **Political Systems and their Relationship to the Economy and Freedom**.

Political Leadership Among People

Since I was a child and throughout my life, I hear people around me complain about the evils of the world and how thing ought to be different.

As I got older and I got more politically involved I have attempted to persuade other people towards more political and in general civic involvement. To that effect I have also started some organizations of my own and wrote what I consider able books on political and economic subjects.

In attempting to get people more involved I discovered, to my surprise, the following:

a. The majority of people do not understand, confront or accept the fact that, there are evil, confused or at best unintelligent people who want to undermine and suppress others. In addition,

b. most of the good and able people in our society are not involved in our political and civic affairs and therefore not contributing their abilities to better our political system.

An example, that covers both of these points is nuclear weapons. I consider nuclear weapons to be the biggest problem on our planet today (sorry it's not global warming). Once explained, most people would agree with the fact that a mishap could turn this planet into a dust ball; but very few people confront this issue and I personally do not know anyone who is actually doing something about it.

Therefore, after extensive observation and historical research, I discovered that very few people will actually do something to improve our world and most people just blame others, especially the politicians, without doing anything to help.

I call the politicians the dance group of the village, city, or country, and not the real leaders of the world. What do they "dance"? The "songs" the citizens are "singing", of course, what else could they be "dancing"? As such the politicians, most of them anyway, take their cue from surveys and observations. They observe what the people actually support, and they offer that every time in order to get elected, what else do you expect them to do? Yet, we constantly hear people blaming the politicians. Well, who voted them in office in the first place? In fact, sometimes the voters will continue to vote for certain politicians even after it is proven that these elected officials lied about things or that they had illegal dealings.

You see, the people always have the power of choice, the power to agree or disagree with what is happening, regardless of what they are told. If you as a citizen want a different action by the politicians then sing them a different song to bring about a change, simple. And here is the interesting part. Who will bring this change? Who will sing a different song? Who among the people will provide the political leadership needed?

What I discovered about this subject after years of research about politics and economics was somewhat disheartening although very real and therefore very enlightening as you will see in the subsequent pages.

I discovered that when it comes to political will, the world is divided into three types of people.

5%	The top 5%
90%	The masses 90%
5%	The bottom 5%

1. *The top **5%** are the **good** and **able** people in any society. They are usually busy creating things to improve their survival potential.*

2. ***90%** are the masses These people are **followers** and will just follow whoever pushes them or mesmerizes them the most. For the most part, they are good people, but are not very brave.*

3. *The bottom **5%** are the bad guys **able** or **unable**. At any given time, 5% of the population is either ill-willed or very confused, but very willing to cause trouble and suppress others. **These bad guys, the bottom 5%, I call them "Chronic Barbarians", are never idle, they are always doing something or supporting a cause which has an ultimate negative result for the rest of us. In short, they always cause trouble.** Even a crazy catatonic person requires a lot of energy from others just to survive.*

As mentioned above, the majority of the people, 90% of them, are unwilling to do anything and certainly unwilling to stand up to ill willed people who create bad effects on others and in general, suppress others. In fact, the masses will not even support the good guys without probing, coaxing and educating them as to why it's good to do so for their own survival.

Thus the burden for optimum survival in any society rests on the shoulders of the top 5% of its citizens. All great movements in our world have been brought about by a desperate few.

If the top 5% are not putting order and commanding the other 95%; then the bottom 5%, the chronic barbarians, by default will run the country. (See troubled countries around the world).

The moral of the story is that the top 5% of the people in any society must constantly lead the country to a better place and they must constantly be actively involved in the political process for their country to do well. These are the people who are endowed with more goodness and observation ability than the rest of their peers. The other guys simply do not have what it takes to confront and lead.

As Pericles, the Father of Democracy in his famous speech "The Epitaph", asserted to the Athenians: For things to be well in the country, the responsible citizens must be constantly involved in the political process and civic affairs.

You ask can we change the other 95%? Well, that's a long answer and not belonging in this book, but my short answer is: **Unfortunately, No!**

At this point I am sure I will lose a lot of readers, but I have one benefit over most professional writers, in that I don't have to support myself from my writings, so I write as I see things. You the reader decide.

To summarize, what I have witnessed in our society is that only the top 5% the good and able people can be persuaded to do something. The next 90% are simply, followers. They will follow the top or bottom 5%, whoever wins, mesmerizes or prods them the most.

People ask me: "How did you come up with this breakdown?" My answer is: "By reading history and by observing life and people in it."

The above categorization also explains the eternal battle we all read or hear about between good and evil. This battle is between the good 5%, and the bad or evil 5%. The battle is constant.

Evil is defined as: Something against optimum survival.

The definition of good: A reach toward optimum survival.

Most people do not want to confront that they are constantly in this battle. Listen to what the majority of people are saying and what they constantly admire. They talk about wanting to relax, have a good time, be at peace, retire, go on vacation, see a movie (turn off reality), see a game, get drunk, take drugs, etc. Do they sound like they want to battle the bad guys? And if they do, they want a God to do the work for them. That is why evil gets strong because the good guys cannot confront it, let along go against it.

*The good news is that under a normal democratic environment this 5% only needs to do minimal things to make the correct changes needed in our society. But **they must do them, and do them constantly**. I know a lot of people whom I would put in the top 5% of our society and believe me when I tell you, they do nothing to alter and help the political processes. They refuse to educate themselves about politics and economics and do very little to help. They talk about cars, houses, girlfriends, boyfriends, and the like, but spend no energy in the political process. The reason? It is because they do not have the data I present in this book and think that they can survive well without a team and without democracy in a free enterprise system. Also, they are not taught to confront* *evil conditions and/or evil people. See next chapter. But if under normal circumstances in a democratic environment,* **you get a small percentage, as little as .3% of the people (1 in 300) to get really involved and do something, pro-survival, things will change for the better.** *What is that something that people can do? It could be as little as a letter to a politician supporting his efforts, whom they perceive as good for the country with a contribution of say $100 and a copy of that letter to the media. In America, that would amount to a contribution of over one hundred million dollars to a politician or organization they support and over a million copies to the media.* **Imagine the effect something like this would have. And imagine if it's done every year.** *That's minimal, yet powerful.*

If on the other hand, 1% of the population or otherwise said 20% of the good guys get really involved, we will then have a golden age.

I also discovered that if only 10% of the people in any society are just vocal about something pro-survival, they will bring about a change, even without doing anything other than just being vocal about a wanted path, action or a change of a condition.

You say: Wow! It only takes so few people in order to bring about a change? The answer is yes, only a few. You see the sad truth is that most people do nothing! Test this in your environment and with your friends and if you find the above to be true, then you have an obligation to enlighten others. Otherwise, we will be run by the bottom 5%, the chronic barbarians. So, get busy and help out. You owe it to your children and future generations. You need to stand up against the bottom 5% for your benefit and everyone else's. If you don't, then you will succumb to the crazies and you will enter the river of Styx and be carried to the underworld, with all the rest of us. This metaphor of the underworld has historically been called "The Dark Ages." **Communism or fascism, no matter their disguises, always bring in dark, very dark ages.**

In the past, people could escape in the forests, islands, mountains or monasteries. Today there is no escape, due to the advent of electronics, satellites and smart bombs. So, get active, fight back and do not allow the dark ages to come in.

Again, if you understand all this, you are one of the top five percent or perhaps higher. If you don't do something about things, no one else will and we will all be doomed. Don't believe the media, they have agendas. The media does not report the news, they create the "news" and we follow.

CHAPTER 21
POLITICAL SYSTEMS AND
THE WESTERN WORLD

The Western World has a misunderstood on the word renaissance. As such, they think that everything about the world was discovered during the renaissance. **Renaissance means rebirth.** In order to be a rebirth, there must first have been a birth. Therefore, the discoveries were done at birth, not at the rebirth. During the renaissance, the Western World discovered what happened at birth, which took place in the Hellenistic world, i.e., Greek Classical Era.

All the political systems including communism, were tried and tested in Greece. Marx did not discover communism; he just rehashed some old Greek ideas of Lycourgos from Sparta, as he interpreted them, while drinking (he was a heavy drinker). The English did not discover Free Enterprise, it has existed since the ancient times. It's innate anyhow.

Therefore, the struggle between freedom and totalitarianism (Free Enterprise vs Socialism) is the struggle of the ages and as such let's not pretend that is something new and different, otherwise we are trying to solve the wrong problem. It has been going on for thousands of years.

It has played out something like this: The freedom advocates start a governing system which is closer to free enterprise and democracy, the country expands, and things are going well. But the system is far from perfect and a lot of mistakes are made, such as the creation of monopolies and big governmental bodies. Injustices then take place and the advocates of totalitarianism find fertile ground to rouses the people to revolt against free enterprise and democracy by calling it by other names such as Capitalism or the rich against the poor or whatever. But these problems and injustices did not come from true free enterprise and proper democracy, but due to the alterations of it.

As such, this struggle between Freedom and Totalitarianism has gone on forever and most of the time the dark forces of totalitarianism have won. America is about to go through this phase as the antifreedom forces are about to overtake its freedom advocates.

The Ancient Greeks fought for freedom and democracy which idea they taught to the Romans who carried it West. The American forefathers copied Athenian Democracy and continued the struggle to win freedom and democracy once again.

America was never perfect, but it became the greatest country **compared** to others. How so? By adopting free enterprise and democracy better than anyone else and it created a society where people had choices, freedom, justice, and the ability to pursue their own spirituality and not be treated like animals. But, today the year 2019, if you ask ten people walking about in any street in America, I doubt if one of them will tell you the above reasons as to why America became the place the world wants to come to. That's a complete failure of the top 5% of our population, the good and able guys and girls on their efforts to keep the country on the straight and narrow road of freedom and democracy.

I say let's put an end to this long struggle between democracy and totalitarianism by creating a True Free Enterprise system, not Capitalism with its monopolies and oligopolies, in a responsible democracy, as fully explained in the book, *What is Wrong with Democracy and How to Fix it.*

If we create such a system, we'll bring about a golden age and diminish the chances of the totalitarian forces to ever overtake us.

I can write about such a system, but you need to support it in order for it to come to fruition.

"A society is headed toward greatness when old people plant trees whose shade they will never use."

-Old Greek Proverb

Chapter 22
FUTURE SOCIETIES, JUSTICE AND FREEDOM

In the future man will go to space, conquer and develop other planets, just as we see in futuristic movies. What you and I don't like about these futuristic films is that they portray societies which are not very democratic, and justice is based on suppressive governments, business monopolies or individual strong man self-interests. As such, these futuristic societies do not look very appealing at all. In fact, they appear to be very scary places to live in. **What is the common thread? Totalitarian political systems with enterprises which are monopolistic conglomerates and in bed with oppressive governments.**

These films portray a future of totalitarian states and economies which suppress individual freedom and individualism and turn people into machines.

It does not have to be this way. We can avert this course if we support and vote for free enterprise and democracy.

Don't be fooled by your apathetic "friends," who say history repeats itself and that all things will come out alright at the end. No, history does not repeat, that's a falsehood. Athens is no longer the center of the world as it was 2,500 years ago. Neither is Rome. Also these apathetic people think that their fellow citizens will ultimately realize their mistakes and that if they support communism and it fails, they will revert back to supporting free enterprise and fix it.

Really? When did this ever happen in history? Once communists are in power, they stay there, and the corruption is rampant. Russia is still run by the communists, over 100 years after the revolutionaries original mistake. **Unfortunately, no great culture on earth has ever come back from the ashes. Once it goes down, its stays there. Yes, there are resurgences but never like its previous self, it's like an almost, lacking its old true flavor.**

So, if you allow your country to be overrun by the barbarians, it will be almost impossible to bring it back to true free enterprise and responsible democracy. The forces of the bad guys will have corrupted people and systems to such an extent that all hope will have vanished.

So, get involved!

The problems people have with politics are:

a. They do not understand the importance of it and **the fact that the political system that exists in a country is what determines its success or failure**. So, they need to read this book.

b. They cannot confront evil or illogics. Meaning that they can't believe that some normal looking people can be so evil or totally illogical (the bottom 5%). But…confront they must, because it is a fact witnessed by history over and over. **Illogical people** or illogical things must be handled as illogical and dealt with as such and not be sugar-coated and pretend that they are something else than what they truly are.

c. They think that someone is handling things for them and no need to supervise their doings as they are "checked" by the opposing party.

In Thucydides' "Epitaph", Pericles (the Famous Athenian Statesman and Father of Democracy) proclaimed that: The people who are not involved in civic life and are not contributing to the democratic process **are not pacifists, but useless.**

We need an enlightened critical mass of educated citizenry. That is the purpose of my books. So, don't be a "pacifist", but pass them on if you agree with what is written in them, otherwise you or your children will find yourselves in a suppressive society controlled by electronics and no justice with no way out.

A Fitting End

The following is an excerpt of a speech Ronal Reagan gave January 20th, 1981 during his first Inaugural Address

"If we look to the answer, as to why for so many years we achieved so much, prospered as no other people on Earth, it was because here in this land we unleashed the energy and individual genius of man to a greater extent than has ever been done before. Freedom and the dignity of the individual have been more available and assured here than in any other place on Earth.

The price for this freedom at times has been high but we have never been unwilling to pay that price. Those who say that we're in a time when there are no heroes — they just don't know where to look. The sloping hills of Arlington National Cemetery, with its row upon row of simple white markers bearing crosses or stars of David, they add up to only a tiny fraction of the price that has been paid for our freedom."

-Ronald Reagan

ABOUT THE AUTHOR

Vienna 2018

Dr. Alemis left Greece in 1975 as he saw the winds of socialism sweeping the country and predicted Greece's downfall way before it happened. He never understood what others saw in socialism and communism and was always suspicious of their promises.

Made in the USA
Monee, IL
30 December 2019

19678616R00125